OPTIONS TRADING

THE EXHAUSTIVE CRASH COURSE

GET YOUR FINANCIAL INCOME

By

Ryan Drake

© **Copyright 2020 by Ryan Drake - All rights reserved.**

This document is geared towards providing exact and reliable information regarding the topic and issue covered. The publication is sold with the idea that the publisher is not required to render accounting, officially permitted, or otherwise, qualified services. If advice is necessary, legal, or professional, a practiced individual in the profession should be ordered. - From a Declaration of Principles which was accepted and approved equally by a Committee of the American Bar Association and a Committee of Publishers and Associations. In no way is it legal to reproduce, duplicate, or transmit any part of this document in either electronic means or in printed format. Recording of this publication is strictly prohibited and any storage of this document is not allowed unless with written permission from the publisher. All rights reserved. The information provided herein is stated to be truthful and consistent, in that any liability, in terms of inattention or otherwise, by any usage or abuse of any policies, processes, or directions contained within is the solitary and utter responsibility of the recipient reader. Under no circumstances will any legal responsibility or blame be held against the publisher for any reparation, damages, or monetary loss due to the information herein, either directly or indirectly. Respective authors own all copyrights not held by the publisher. The information herein is offered for informational purposes solely and is universal as so. The presentation of the information is without a contract or any type of guarantee assurance. The trademarks that are used are without any consent, and the publication of the trademark is without permission or backing by the trademark owner. All trademarks and brands within this book are for clarifying purposes only and are owned by the owners themselves, not affiliated with this document.

TABLE OF CONTENTS

Introduction 1

Chapter 1: Getting Started With Options Trading 5

Chapter 2: Call And Put As Options Trading Fundamental ... 21

Chapter 3: Basic Option Trading Strategies 27

Chapter 4: Methods Of Buying Options 34

Chapter 5: Back Spread Strategy In Options Trading 41

Chapter 6: Intrinsic And Time Value In Options Trading 47

Chapter 7: Inter-Market Analysis In For Retail Asset Allocation 53

Chapter 8: Weekly Options Trading 59

Chapter 9: Trade Performance Metrics Portfolio Measures 68

Chapter 10: Vertical Spread Strategy 79

Chapter 11: Getting A Trading Edge In Options Trading 86

Chapter 12: Evaluation Of Variables In Option Prices 97

Chapter 13: Analyzing Market Trends In Options Trading . 104

Chapter 14: The Basics Of Trading Stock Options 110

Chapter 15: Understanding Stock Option Contracts 116

Chapter 16: Advantages Of Trading Scheme Leverage Options 124

Chapter 17: Choosing The Right Options Brokers 129

Chapter 18: Premium Selling For Low Maintenance Options Trading 136

Chapter 19: Options For Flexible Instruments 142

Chapter 20: Options Trading Using Arbitrage 152

Chapter 21: Is Stock Options Trading Risky? 158

Chapter 22: Thinking "Outside The Box" 164

Chapter 23: How To Get Maximum Profits In Less Time On Your Option Trades 170

Chapter 24: Attributes Of A Successful Options Trader 178

Chapter 25: Tenets Of Daily Trade Discipline In Options Trading 185

Chapter 26: Ways To Improve Your Options Trading 193

Conclusion 200

INTRODUCTION

Before I wrote this CRASH COURSE on OPTIONS TRADING, I thought I should check the Internet to see what information was on options trading. I was shocked to find that little was posted on the subject. Really!

There are hundreds of websites, brokerage firms, and business providers that want to offer their product to you. The reality is that very few can explain what a trading network is in fact.

At its root, option trading systems are a way of producing signals for buy and sell using a proven stock analysis tool. The program can be based on any form of optional strategy and includes both basic and technical analysis.

Options trading may concentrate on changes in the underlying stock price, leverage, time depreciation, unusual buy/sell behavior, or a combination of these components.

Essentially, it is a set of conditions that must be met before joining companies. When all conditions are met, a signal is produced to buy or sell. The criteria for each type of option trading strategy are different.

Each one has its own trading system model, whether it is long calls, covered calls, spreads, or selling naked index options. A salt-worthy Option Trading Program can allow you to remove false signals and create trust in entries and exits.

The demand for options is very complex. Without a program, options trading is like constructing a house without a strategy. Volatility, time, and movement of stocks can all impact your profitability. You must be mindful of each of these variables.

When the market changes, it's easy to be swayed by emotions. With a device, your response to those very real and usual emotions can be regulated. How much did you sit and watch a trade losing money while your order was fulfilled?

Or, have you ever seen a stock price surge wondering whether or not you should buy it?

It is important to have a clear strategy in place for sound and rational trade decisions. You can boost your business operations emotionlessly and automatically by designing and implementing a successful program.

Selling Options gives the stock market leverage. With options, hundreds or thousands of stock shares can be managed at a fraction of the stock price itself. A shift of five to ten percent in stock prices will lead to a rise of one hundred percent or more.

Seek to focus the trade on percentage gains over dollar losses. It needs a radical shift in traditional thought, but for an effective trading system to be controlled, it is necessary.

The trading of good options reduces the risk in two essential ways. Cost is the first method. The price of the options is very small compared to the buying of the same stock. The second way issues end. A successful system easily reduces losses and keeps them low.

The more tools in your toolbox, the more likely you are to change the markets. If the market were to act similarly every day, trading would be a play for children.

You must build a trading strategy or blueprint to lead you in the right direction to start designing your options trading program. Start with a simple framework and tweak it to evaluate and develop your trading criteria.

If an options trading system were like a tic-tac-toe scheme, we would all be rich. Fortunately, option trading isn't as dull as a child's game. Endeavor to learn the strategies discussed in this GUIDE and apply it in your trading program of options.

Are you ready?

Let's get started

CHAPTER 1
GETTING STARTED WITH OPTIONS TRADING

An Option is a legal arrangement between the buyer and seller to buy or sell security within a specified time at an agreed price. It's very similar to insurance where you pay an amount of money so that the insurance provider covers your house.

The distinction between the two is the insurance policy cannot be sold, but it can be exchanged. Two forms of option contracts exist; call options and put options.

We buy the call option when we assume that the safety price will rise and buy the option if the security price is expected to decrease. We may also sell the call if the security price is expected to drop and vice versa if we offer the call option.

The option is usually counted by contract, with one contract corresponding to 100 options for units. 1 unit right covers the share of 1 trade. One contract, therefore, covers 100 unit shares.

The language that you should know before learning how to trade is as follows:

a) Strike price: Strike price is the value that both the purchaser and the seller of the option agree on. This means that if the call option's strike price is 35, the seller of this option obliges the buyer of the option to sell protection at this price even if the protection price on the market is more than 35 when the buyer exercises this right.

This choice can be purchased by the buyer at a price lower than the market price. The buyer will receive $4 if the current market price is $39. Unless the security price is lower than the impact price, the buyer shall retain the option and cancel the option of expiring without interest.

The buyer of the option shall be entitled to sell the

security to the seller of the option at the strike price. This means that, if the price of the option is 30 then the seller of this option must purchase the security from the buyer at that price when he or she exercises the opportunity even if the price of the market is lower than that price.

If the price is $25, the buyer would be liable for $5. It seems that several transactions have taken place, but ultimately, the seller does not buy a security and sell it to the buyer.

The broker trade does all the purchases, but the extra money used to buy the security must be paid by the seller. And if the seller loses 4 dollars, the purchaser will receive 4 dollars.

b) Out of cash, cash, and near / by the money option: the price of the option includes the value of time and the intrinsic price.

The market value is the amount of money that the option is worth regardless of the time the option has until its expiry date. The longer the length of the contract, the higher the time value of the contract. If the option has expired, the time value of an option will be zero.

The difference between the actual market security price and the option strike price is the intrinsic value of the money call contract.

Conversely, the difference between the contract price and the actual market security price is the inherent value of the money set contract. If the actual price for coverage is cheaper than the price of a call option, the option is a non-money option. It only has a meaning of time.

Calling with a strike price below the current security price is a choice for capital. Every choice has both time value and intrinsic value. The option, whose strike price is close to, or near, the current market security price, is the money option.

c) Delta value: Delta value indicates that when a security price changes to $1,00 the price of the option will change. That is a positive call option value and a negative call option value. It varies between 0.1 and 1.0. Delta value is more than 0.5 for the money alternative, and less than 0.5 for the money alternative.

The deep delta value in the cash option normally exceeds 0.9. If the delta value of the option is 0.6, which means that the security price increases by $1, the option price will increase by $0.60. If the protection price increases by 0,10, $the option price increases by 0,06$. $0.06 is normally up to $0.10.

d) Theta value: Theta value is a negative value that indicates the time value decline of the option. The option which has longer expiry time has a lower absolute theta value than the option that has a shorter expiry time.

Strong absolute value Theta means the time value of the option decays faster than the absolute low-value Theta. A theta value of -0.0188 means that after seven days, the option will lose $0.0188 of its premium. Options with a low absolute value are better for purchase than options with a high absolute value for theta.

e) Gamma value: the gamma value signals a shift in the option delta value as the protection price rises or decreases. For example, the gamma value of 0.03 means that this option's delta value increases by 0.03 when the security price increases by $1.

The alternative, which has a longer expiry time, has less gamma value than the alternative that has a shorter expiry time. The Gamma value also changes significantly as the security price moves close to the option hit price.

f) Vega value: Vega value indicates the shift in option value in the implied volatility by one percent. This is also a positive thing. Near to the money alternative, the Vega value is higher than in cash and money.

The option that has longer expiry time has a higher vega value than the option that has a shorter expiry time. Given that vega value tests the sensitivity of the option for increasing safety uncertainty, higher vega value options than low vega value options are preferable to buy.

g) Implied volatility: the theoretical meaning is implied volatility, which is used to describe a security price volatility. The real option price, security price, option strike price, and option expiration date is determined by replacing them with the Black-Scholes equation. High-volatility options cost more than low-volatility options.

This is because the share with a high volatility stock is more likely to be in the money share until its expiry. Most investors prefer high stock volatility options rather than low stock volatility options.

In fact, there are 21 options trading, which most investors and traders use in their regular trading. I am only implementing ten policies as follows, however: a) naked appeal or put b) call or put spread d) strand d) strand e) covered appeal f) collar g) condor h) butterfly spread j) calendars

Naked appeal and meaning to buy and place a call at a strike price is similar to the market safety level. If the security price increases, the advantage is to deduct the security price to the strike price if you buy a call and the reverse is if you buy a call.

Calling and putting spread is accomplished by buying money or by selling the money alternative. When the security price rises, you generate income from the money call option you purchase, and the money you sell loses money.

However, because of the delta value differential, the price of the money call option rises as the security price increases at a higher rate relative to the out-of-money call option.

You still gain money when you subtract the income from the loss. The object of selling the money option is to cover the time value deterioration of the cash call option if the security price decreases.

But if the security price continuously falls, there would be an infinite loss. Stopping failure must, therefore, be set at a certain point. This strategy also has a maximum benefit if the security price in the money option strike price has been passed over.

Straddle will earn money regardless of the up or down security price. This strategy is built by buying near the cash call and placing the option at the same price. The downside to this technique is the high degree to breakdown.

The sum of the call and the right to request price is the breakthrough stage of this strategy. You earn income even when the security price is higher or lower than the breakdown.

If the safety price fluctuates in the bottom and top, you still lose money. The money you lose is due to the value of the option period.

This strategy is typically enforced for protection, which is highly volatile or before the earnings report is published. The overall loss of this strategy is the total call and place price. In both sides of the market, this approach will produce infinite income.

Strangle's pretty much like straddle.

The difference is odd by buying the money call and

putting alternatives. Since both options are out of the cash system, both options have a different effect. The overall loss is less than the straddle strategy, while the gap between up and down is marginally higher than the straddle strategy.

The upside breakeven is estimated for this strategy by adding the total call and set option prices on the call option strike price. In addition, the disadvantage level is determined by extracting the set option price from the total call and set option prices.

The difference between strike prices is usually about 2.50 or 5 depending on the stock you want to buy with this strategy. If the security price fluctuates at the upside and down, the loss of the time value of the option still causes you to lose the money. This technique is being implemented in the same way as the straddle technique.

Call coverage is rendered by buying a security at the current market request rates and selling the money call option. The selling of the cash option restricted the benefit that this strategy generated. If the security price declines continuously, the loss is infinite. Stop loss must, therefore, be set.

When the option expires, if the security price doesn't dramatically increase, you also get the same option premium you received. When the price of protection rises, you can likely gain a small income.

If the stock price falls continuously, there would be an infinite loss. Stop loss must, therefore, be set. Usually, stop loss is set at the security request price after the option bid price has been subtracted.

If this security price falls and goes above the price you set as a stop loss, the loss you get is approximately half the total option premium you got. The delta value of the money call option that you offered is roughly 0.4 – 0.5. The price of the cash call option must be the closest price to the entrant security price.

Collar is also known as the covered medium call. It is quite similar to the call strategy protected. Just one step more is added to make stop-loss unnecessary in this technique.

This strategy is characterized by purchasing security and selling a money option close to the capital. Due to the product you have purchased, it is needless to set a stop loss as the security product protects if the security price is that.

The money choice premium you receive will also be used to pay the charge for the service. If the security price drops, you still lose about half of the overall premium for the put option. That is because the cash call premium is smaller than the closest cash price. This approach is for a long-term investment of half or one year.

There are four variations of the Condor strategy.

Two for the stable market and two for the dynamic (volatile) market.

Long condors and calls are for the stationary market, while short calls and calls are for the dynamic market.

The former strategy involves four measures, in which money and the money call option are purchased and sold with an equal contract number. This strategy will produce income as long as the security price does not fluctuate at the ups and downs. Short condors for the competitive market require four phases, like the long condor strategy.

The difference is that the strike prices for the options purchased will start at the strike prices of the options offered in a short condor call. For short calls and condor strategies, profit can be generated as long as the security price has fluctuated from the upside to the downside.

The upside split is determined by applying the total place pay-out or by getting the highest strike price in the strategy. The disadvantage amount is determined by eliminating the total place pay or by getting the lowest strike price of the strategy.

The Combo strategy consists of two combinations which are bullish and bearish. Bullish combo strategy is for the bullish market and the combination strategy for bearish is for the bearish market. This strategy consists of two stages, the purchasing of capital and the selling of capital. If the security price rises above the higher price, profit can be generated.

However, if the safety price falls below the lower strike price, there would be a loss. When the price of safety fluctuates at the higher and lower rate, you're not going to risk anything. This strategy will produce unlimited income, but also unlimited losses depending on the size of your business and the technique you have used.

Butterfly propagation strategy is similar to the condor strategy. It also has four variations that are long on the cash call and spread butterflies and short on the cash call and spread butterflies. Long at the money call and spread of butterfly is for stationary and short at the cash call and spread of butterfly is for volatile business.

Measures that take a long time spreading the money call butterfly are the money and money call option and then sell the money call option. With the cash option, the striking price of this option is similar to the current consumer safety price. The number of contracts of the choice at the cash call will equal the number of contracts of the money choice in and out.

Benefit can be produced as long as the price for protection doesn't switch upside down. By adding the total pay from this position to the highest rate, the upside breaks are determined. The downside divisive is determined by subtracting the lowest strike price from this position with the total pay.

The breakdown at the money call butterfly is decided by selling the money call option in and out and then buying the money call option. Contract numbers of the money option will be twice as many as in and out of the money option.

As long as the price of security is upside-down and downside, profit can be created. This approach produces limited benefits and also results in a limited loss if the safety price is not pushed in the right direction.

The distribution of the calendar is also known as

horizontal or distribution of time. It is only used to gain money from the protection that trades prices on the side. There are many stocks with a price pattern of this nature.

This strategy is created by selling money or placing an option that has a shorter period to end and buying money and putting an option that has a longer time to expire. This technique only raises money from the option's time value.

The shorter expiry-term option depreciates the time value quicker than the expiry-time option. The alternative that has a shorter expiry period is usually left to expire worthlessly. The total money you get after this role is more than the total money you paid out when you opened it.

With these strategies, you will gain money from the upside and downside market, as well as the sideways market.

CHAPTER 2
CALL AND PUT AS OPTIONS TRADING FUNDAMENTAL

Commonly, stocks are transacted into blocks that are separated by 100. A round lot has long been a regular trading unit for public exchanges. We have the right on the stock exchange to purchase and sell infinite quantities of shares as long as people can buy at the seller's fixed price.

They typically set their commissions for a trade for a total of 100 units of share at a certain price for a brokerage trade. If we buy less than 100 share units, they still place this tax on us.

For example, if we buy 100 units and pay USD 30 for buying and selling transactions to the brokerage firm, they charge us this amount also: USD 30 when we buy and sell only 1 unit of share.

The fee the brokerage business pays for the stock

sale varies from one stock to another. Some brokerage companies can charge less, but you have to trade a lot in a single contract. Each choice unit, therefore, represents 100 share units.

In reality, there are two types of calling and placing options. The call option gives its owner the right, within a period, to buy 100 units of share of a trade at a defined price negotiated between its owner and the seller. If the stock price rises, then during this time, the call option price will also rise and vice versa. The second choice is to position the choice.

This option gives the owner the right, within a period, to sell 100 shares of an undertaking at a fixed price negotiated between the proprietor and the seller of the option. Put tends to be the opposite of call choice. If the stock price rises during this time, the price of the put option decreases. You can either buy or sell the call or put option.

As long as people can sell, people are willing to buy. There are four permutations available during an option transaction. The first is to buy a call option that allows you to buy 100 shares. Secondly, the call option means that you sell the right to buy 100 units to someone else from you.

The third one is to purchase an option, which means you can buy the right to sell 100 units of shares. The last is to sell an option which means that you have the right to sell 100 units of shares to someone else.

The other way to explain these differences is to bear in mind that the buyer of the call option expects the stock prices will rise and the option buyer will aim for a decrease in the price per share. On the other hand, a calling option seller hopes that the stock price will stay or decline. Whereas, the option seller hopes that the inventory price will increase.

When the buyer of options, irrespective of the calls or choice, forecasts the price movement of the stock correctly, he or she will benefit from his decision. In addition to predicting the course of stock price movement, there is another barrier to choice.

This obstacle is that the price of the stock will adjust before the option deadline. As a stockholder, we might forecast long-term prospects for a stock by waiting for a long-term stock shift. However, we may not have that kind of potential for the option holder.

This is because options are endless; in a short time, they lose all their interest, usually within a few months. It has long-term options, however, which can last for up to one to three years. Despite this constraint, time would be a significant factor in deciding whether or not an option investor will make a profit.

In the first place, the choice is to give the buyer an unconditional right to purchase or sell 100 share units at the negotiated price between the buyer and the seller of the choice. The right is therefore just an arrangement for 100 share units of a specific stock and a certain price per share.

Therefore, if the buyer buys an option at the wrong time, the buyer will make no profit. False timing ensures that when the deadline has passed, the stock price does not rise or does not rise substantively. When we buy a call option, it would appear that we agree that we are willing to pay the price at which a contractual right has to be paid.

The right offered that we can buy 100 share units at a fixed cost per share, and this right is there when we purchased the option until the option's deadline. When we acquired the option before the date of the contract, this call option will become valuably more attractive if the stock price is higher than the fixed price indicated in the option agreement.

Just think that we buy a call option which gives us the right to purchase 100 share units at USD 70 per share. Let us claim that the stock price per share was up to USD 90 per share before the option deadline. As the holders of this call option, we are entitled to buy 100 share units at USD 70, which is USD 20 lower than the market price currently applied.

It is the case when stock market values surpass the agreed contract prices stated in the call option agreement. Here, as the buyer, we will be entitled to purchase 100 units, which is USD 20 less than the current market price.

While we have the right to do so, we will conduct our right unnecessarily. For instance, how about when the stock price has dropped to USD 50?

At a fixed price of USD 70, we would not have to buy shares and we may agree not to take any action.

CHAPTER 3

BASIC OPTION TRADING STRATEGIES

If you are new to options trading, by now, you probably already know how to buy puts and calls. Those are the two most relevant options and the ones to which novice options traders are inclined. That makes sense.

Transfers are risk-free and understandable. Buy a place and you want to decrease the underlying security. Buy a call and you're allowing the underlying security to increase. In any case, risk exposure is limited to the price you pay to buy the trade. If the contract ends without interest, you will just lose the cost of the contract.

To this end, we are certainly fans of buying calls, regardless of how experienced your preference level is. In the investing world, the potential for massive returns without the need to bet the farm on any transaction is unequaled.

Yet we do want to extend our horizons and invest in options is one of the best ways to do so. With so many different choices, there is always a way to benefit literally.

Let's look at the top ten choices.

1. The Protected Call

Writing options allow us to sell an option contract that, in certain cases, may be risky, but not protected. Indeed, covered call writing is probably the most conservative option because your ownership of the underlying stock is the protection of the contract you write.

Let's presume that you own 500 highly liquid blue-chip shares like Microsoft. Microsoft is not very unpredictable, making it the perfect applicant for protected call publishing. It is a smart idea to make calls to inventories that are not highly volatile so we can make out of - the money calls and increase income in the form of a premium. Think Microsoft's $23 trading.

We could write calls for the $25 strike for the contract next month. The danger, in this case, is that if the basic stock reaches the strike price before expiry, the call buyer may withdraw our stock at $25, which is the discount on the market price.

You can see why you are sponsored by the inventory and why you want to pick inventories linked to the selection. As a general rule, one call contract will be written for every 100 shares of the underlying firm.

2. Married Put

Married trade is another relatively conservative strategy. Married vouchers are just like covered calls since you own the underlying stock already and you can buy the sum of vouchers equal to your own number.

You will be on the puts for a long time here, but because you possess the base stock, the puts are the shield. In other terms, you will make money if the stock declines.

3. The Bull Call

A variety of different choices, known as spreads, exist. One of the most important is the distribution of the bull call. You purchase telephone calls at a single strike price and sell the same number of calls at a higher strike price.

And you can sell five Microsoft 27.50 or 30 calls if you bought five Microsoft 25 calls. The contracts will expire the same month and the underlying protection for the trade to be used as a bull call. It's a sumptuous plan.

4. The bear put

The bull's bearish relative is the wolf. Here you're buying puts for one strike price and then sell a low strike price for the same sum of puts. Both techniques restrict profits, but also reduce losses.

5. As you can see, many options strategies provide investors with security. The security collar is another of these trades.

You can buy a cash-post option with a protective

collar, and write (or sell) an out of-of - the-money call option with the same protection. This strategy is being used by investors who have already gained substantial appreciation from the underlying security as a way to lock income.

6. The Long Straddle

Got the impression that a stock is making a major move, but you don't know how the move is going?

That's cool because you both buy a put and call at the same price and the same security expiry. This is known as a long straddle and you are perfectly positioned to take advantage of a major move, irrespective of the direction.

7. The Long Strangle

The long strangle, but with this trade, is a twist. You'll buy a put and a call with the same security with the same end date but at different strike rates with a long strangle.

A strangle is typically a little cheaper than a straddle because you buy the money. Your loss is limited to the expense charged for trade with both long straddles and strangles.

8. The Butterfly spreading is an advanced options technique that may seem challenging to the investor with novice options.

We blend bullish and bearish spreads using three separate price ranges in a butterfly spread. One example of a butterfly spread would be to buy the lowest or the highest available strike price, then purchase two of the products that we did not buy in the first level, at higher or lower strike prices.

Let's try to make understanding this quick. Buy one call, buy two puts, and add another call. Voila, the butterfly is spreading.

9. The Iron Condor

Another special options strategy targeted more at seasoned traders in options is the iron condor. The iron condor is dangerous and complicated because you are in two strangles at the same time keeping a long and short spot. This is the kind of trade you need to study before spending money on it randomly.

10. The Iron Butterfly

And our final choices are another butterfly, we think you should know. The iron butterfly helps investors to mix a long or a short straddle with a strangle buying or selling. We use all sets of AND calls with the iron butterfly, not one. Using out-of-the-money options it is advised to reduce costs and risks.

CHAPTER 4

METHODS OF BUYING OPTIONS

Of course, choosing the right option strike price and date of expiration can be very difficult. Thus, most buyers of options end up falling flat on their hands ... And they end up losing their trades money.

Are you wasting money because you buy too much or not enough time?

Do you see the price of the stock shift in the direction you expected, but still lose the trade?

Look, there is an options trading learning curve, and if you have replied yes to all of these questions, that is all right. Nobody was born with a knowledge of trade options; everyone was taught to learn and to trade the markets.

For many, this means learning from errors (AKA pays your tuition on the market, in the form of commercial losses).

Furthermore, I would not be honest if I told you I had not paid my fair share of tuition in the past. But I'd like to think I graduated ... And I'm prepared to share a few things I've heard about purchasing options with you.

1. If you buy options, you're not just selling. Most new investors think they're going to make money if they buy a call and the stock price rises. And they're going to make money if they buy a put, and the price drops. Right! Right!

2. There are several components in which an option is priced. Particularly, the price movements of the stock, the selected optional price, the time to expire, and the implicated volatility. The price model choice is simply a probability model.

3. The intrinsic value and extrinsic value are an option.

Example:

FACEBOOK closed on April 1, 2014, at 62.62 The

middle price for the 4/4/14 call (expiry) is $2.01 Intrinsic value would be true if the option were hypothetical today.

The intrinsic value in this case is $1.62.

The extrinsic value is the variable time and volatility.

That is $2.01 minus $1.62 or $0.39 in this situation.

The average price for the 4/4/14 telephone call (expired) $62.5 is $1.04, the intrinsic value of $0.12, and the alien value of $0.92. As you can see, the time and uncertainty of this option are much of the interest.

Note, all options are left with their intrinsic value at expiration.

It's just another way to suggest that they either expire in the cash or expire without any interest.

That will result in 88 percent of its present value losing if the stock settled at $62.62. Just three days after expiration can you see how easily these options consume time and uncertainty.

4. Intrinsic interest is just in-the-money options. That

said, money and out-of-the-money options have international value only. The higher an option is, the more the price of the option shifts with the underlying stock.

An option in the amount can travel with the stock, but it has to overcome (accelerating) the time value ... If the option volatility increases, the option can gain value ... Or if option volatility decreases, the option can lose value.

5. Options trading is classified almost term as "trading gamma," and further (in time) options trading are classified as "trading vega." What does that mean? What does that mean? If you pick short-term options to be acquired, you bet more in the directional change of the stock.

You not only make a bet on the path of the stock if you pick more options, but you also bet the option volatility increases. (The Greek Vega option tests volatility sensitivity).

In reality, there are many mistakes here. If you buy

money or money options, you need to step in a direction to solve the time decline ... And you need to increase optional variance.

If you buy an option, you're still a long vega (or volatility option).

After a benefit announcement, a good example would be ... Volatility option is crushed in almost all situations; often too much ... it overcomes the stock benefit heading in your direction, which eventually makes the option a loser.

6. When we reach maturity, the time value still accelerates. Moreover, the volatility option is a wild card. It can be driven by a variety of factors.

For instance:

Uncertainty-The volatility choice is often increased in biopharmaceutical companies if they have a pending announcement on product approval. The market doesn't know whether the news is good or poor ... However, they fear it's going to trigger a monster-size change to the stock price.

MannKind (MNKD) is a recent example. The stock traded at about $4 per share on 1 April 2014. The $4 calls and puts, which expired on 4/4/14, cost + /- $2,40.

Following closure, their diabetes drug obtained FDA approval and the stock price was more than 100% hours hourly. On the next day of trade, optional stability was destroyed by uncertainty.

Supply & Demand- This is typically due to uncommon choices. For instance, Gastar Exploration Inc (GST) saw the regular 7.5x volume of options on 1 April 2014.

This demand for options triggered an enormous increase in the implied volatility of the options.

The implied volatility increased by over 21,2%.

On the other hand, as major optional sellers enter the market, the value of the premium option decreases, and implied volatility decreases.

7. The higher the implicated uncertainty, the more costly an alternative. The cheaper an option is the lower the implied volatility is. Delta is the Greek option

which shows us how far we expect the stock price movement option to rise.

For example, if we have a 50-delta call option and the stock increases by $1, we can expect to make $0.50. Keep in mind that we're going to lose some time to decline capital.

We will also make money if implicit volatility increases or if implied volatility reduces we will lose money.

Ultimately, you want to swap deltas if you are using options to make directional bets. Ideally, you would like to reduce as much as possible the time value and the volatility variable.

CHAPTER 5

BACK SPREAD STRATEGY IN OPTIONS TRADING

An option is a very common derivative, as its price is less costly than other derivatives like the future. The stock of a blue-chip is a very flexible stock but very expensive. However, by buying the blue-chip stock option we might make a profit just like buying the stock.

Investment and options trading seems like buying stocks. Because of the time value and expiry date of the contract, however, the buying of the naked contract is extremely risky.

If the stock price goes down a lot after you purchase the naked option, after a certain time, even though the stock price is higher, the option price will still be below the demand price you used to buy this option.

This is why we need an investment strategy or trade

alternative. An option is a very effective method for investment and stock trading. By using the option, we could make use of the stock that moves up, down, and up. In addition, the option may also be used to execute an arbitrage strategy to gain a benefit, irrespective of the stock price up, down, or sideways.

The back spread is one of the most common option trading strategies. This strategy is similar to the so-called big and small gambling in China. When we play big and the three dices after we shook and open show that the overall point is high, we will win 1-fold of money.

This means that if we stake 100, we can get another 100 back. Yet we're going to lose 100 if we lose. The back spread strategy is pretty similar to this game. It means that if we spend 1000 USD, we can get another 1000 USD or a 1000 USD loss staked in it.

The estimated profit and loss is $1000. This has been remedied. You're not going to risk any more. The back spread is simply the reverse of the standard spread. The biggest benefit and loss is not necessarily the same. Often it varies a little and depends on the current stock price.

This strategy can be applied through the purchase of the money option and the selling of the money option. Since the price of the in-the-money option is greater than the out-of-the-money option, it is enough for the money earned by selling the out-of-the-money option.

But we do still have to position a deposit in our trading account and the sum is usually the maximum loss that you will suffer if the stock price goes the other way. And if we expect the stock price to rise soon, we will buy the option of money and wealth.

On the other hand, if we expect the inventory price to fall soon, we will buy the cash and cash call option. We seek an example just to be easy to understand. The following table shows a list of MMM business stock put options that expire on Apr 07.

Table 1: List of MMM client stock put options.

The latest stock price is USD 80.94. The choice to use

the striking price is more than the current price and the price is less than the current price. If we expect the stock price to rise soon, we will purchase one 80 Put Option (MMMPP) contract and sell one 85 Put Option (MNZPQ) contract.

If we sell an option, we obtain a sum equal to the tender price, multiplied by the number of units purchased. The amount of money earned per option for a unit is USD 5.2, while the amount of money that we will pay per option for a unit is USD 2.7.

Therefore, the net amount in your trading account is USD 2.5 per unit option after implementing this strategy. This means that your trading account must contain a USD 250 net.

Maximum profit/loss is as follows: maximum benefit = in - the-money bid price-Out - of-the-money option ask price Maximum loss = (top-level strike price = lower strike price)-(the in-the-money option bid price, out-of-the-money option ask price)

The bid price is USD 5.2 and the bid price out of

money is USD 2.7. After both values have been replaced in the above calculations, we should learn that the maximum benefit is USD 2.5, and the maximum loss is USD 2.5.

If we, therefore, purchase one contract for each option in and out of money, the maximum benefit is USD 250, and maximum loss also amounts to USD 250. Breakeven point = Higher strike price = maximum benefit, or breakthrough points = lower strike price + maximum loss may be used to determine the breakthrough point of that strategy.

In this case, the point of breakeven is 82.5. If the stock price rises above 82.5, we will benefit from this strategy. We will gain the full benefit only if we hold the position until the expiry date.

If we sell before the expiry date, we cannot make the full profit. But we can still earn money, just a little less than if we can hold the work until the expiry date. This is because the time value of the sell-out option is not fully acquired.

By using this option trading strategy, you will make a profit as long as your forecast accuracy is greater than 50%. This means that you have to be accurate for at least six bets in 10 bets. The highest continuous loss from here is four times.

Therefore, in order not to lose all your money until you can't start playing, you need to keep 4 or more money back up. And, if you lose a bet, you still have the money to stake on the next bet continually.

And as long as you can retain more than 50 percent of your prediction accuracy, your money will continue to rise. Therefore, if you are interested in learning more about options trading strategy, just go through our website and we will show you how to maximize your income.

CHAPTER 6

INTRINSIC AND TIME VALUE IN OPTIONS TRADING

An option call is defined as "at money" when the underlying security price and the impact price of the option are the same or very similar. For example, let us assume that XYZ is trading at $50.00 per share, and XYZ is trading at $2.00 per contract for 1 month for the $50 call strike option. Please notice that option premiums are per share and each contract includes 100 shares.

The call option buyer has the right to purchase the shares at $50.00 in this case. With XYZ exchanging shares at $50.00, this right does not have an intrinsic value.

The option premium is made up of the full-time interest of XYZ selling at $50.00 per share and a call strike price of 50. If the share value does not Increase over 1 month, the time value variable decreases and the option expires without benefit.

A call option is called "out of the market" when the stock is less than the impact price. For example, a 1-month call option with a 50-strike can be exchanged at 30 cents if shares of an underlying security trading are $45.00 per share of XYZ.

By purchasing the call option, the holder of the option has the right to acquire $50 of the basic security. This option is called "Out of the Market" and has no intrinsic value because of the current stock trading at 45 dollars.

With the share price at $45, there is a time premium for the 50-strike contract. As with the "At the Money" option, the option expires worthless if the share value does not reach the strike price by the expiration date.

A call option is called "in the cash" if the stock is higher than the strike price. When XYZ trades $55 per share, a call with a 50-stroke and 1 month-to-end call option may have a premium of $5.50. In this case, the caller is entitled to own the stock at $50.

With XYZ selling at $55 per share, the intrinsic value of the call option is 5.00. With a $50 strike and $55 XYZ trading, it is possible to split the $5,50 premium into two components.

By extracting the strike price from the stock price we will calculate that the value of the option is 5.00. We then deduct from the premium the intrinsic value to calculate the time value of $0.50 in that case.

A place option is referred to as 'at the money' when the underlying price and the strike price of the option are equal to or similar to that.

With XYZ selling at 50 dollars a share, the pitch option may be exchanged in 50 dollars for 1 month, but with the put purchaser's right to sell at 50 dollars, since the share value is equivalent to the pitch price, there is no intrinsic value.

The 1,90 price of the option is a time premium that ensures that if the share value is not lower than the strike price, the option expires without interest.

A "Out of the Cash" option is considered when the share value of the underlying security is higher than the strike price. With XYZ trading at $55,00 per share, XYZ will trade at 25 cents for 1 month with a 50-dollar strike price.

In this situation, the investor has the right to sell XYZ shares at $50, but the value of this option does not exist since the shares are already trading at $55. The share price is 55 dollars and a 50-cent rise makes the 25-cent premium absolutely of the time value. If the share value remains higher than $50, the put option will expire without value.

A put option is described as "in the money" where the value of the underlying share is lower than the strike price. With XYZ at 45 dollars a share, a 50-stroke option can be sold at $5.40 for 1 month before the expiry date. The buyer has the right to sell the stock at 50.00 dollars even though XYZ is priced at 45.00 dollars.

By extracting the share value from the strike price, we calculate the intrinsic value of the put option. The

50-dollar effect minus the share value of $45 represents an intrinsic value of 5.00 The 5.40 premium can be split into two parts.

After eliminating the 5,00 intrinsic value, the time value portion of the option premium can be estimated to be.40cents. When the share value remains the same, the time value portion depreciates to zero leaving only the intrinsic value.

As with the call option, if a "money put" has an intrinsic or real interest at its expiration, it will exercise automatically. Which choice to use would depend on the trader or investor's objectives. There are some advantages and disadvantages to each type of option.

An "at the money" option represents an inherent value when the underlying options start to move in the expected direction. These options are typically the most liquid and the downside is that from a time value point of view they are the most costly.

And how do you make the right choice?

The options "Out of the Money" require the

minimum amount of capital and offer the most leverage to the investor or trader. However, to realize an intrinsic value, a greater step is required in the underlying. The time portion of the premium would erode even faster. Thus, options for "out of the money" are more likely to expire without interest.

The option "In the money" would cost more as the inherent value is added to the premium's time value. Because the "in the pocket" option is more costly, the consumer has a less leveraged position.

The downside of an "In the money" option is that it needs more capital to be purchased and can very easily lose its value with an adverse change in the underlying security. As the intrinsic value decreases, it accelerates depreciation.

CHAPTER 7

INTER-MARKET ANALYSIS IN FOR RETAIL ASSET ALLOCATION

Even if you allocate capital to the Dow's smaller versions: DJX, the DIA version settled in European style and settled in American style is cash. In addition, if you expand the capital allocation to trade with the RUT to diversify into small capital stocks and away from big firms, you can only fall into shareholdings more of your trading capital.

Again, diversification cannot be accomplished by adding more resources to the same asset class. You must learn how to trade options without stock concentration risk. Do not confuse the asset group with the asset class.

This is where intermarket partnerships ought to be understood. A simultaneous analysis is expected of four main asset classes: currencies, commodities, bonds, and stocks (U.S. dollar remains the most liquid of all key currencies traded). The coordination of asset allocation turnover within your own portfolio lies in how these four markets interrelate.

This is the description of the relationships. Commodities have leading bonds, stocks leading shares, and commodities leading stocks. At least in a normal inflationary/disinflationary setting, the process applies. Apart from themselves, commodities influence 2 markets (Bonds and Stocks); affecting effectively 3 of 4 intermarket relationships.

Even if you do not trade ETFs as part of your portfolio, you must watch commodities as a leading indicator of the economic cycle. The futures / mini futures you see on news headlines/trading screens are only important as daily bond measurements. They are not an asset class period predictor.

You can therefore already understand the parameters for determining a "natural" economic cycle to function in the management relationships (see below); but how do you decide which asset class drives the cycle?

This means how do you assess which asset class has the relative strength to trade in the DOMINANT at a specific point in the inter-market cycle? Follow the link below to learn how the Relative Strength-a rotational algorithmic metric is used as an asset management tool to replace the traditional fundamental analysis.

Moving on, this is, in brief, the market cycle. Bonds lead stocks to a trend in the same direction, except when bonds rise and stocks fall during deflation. On average, bonds are 18 months ahead of stocks that rise or fall to their deposits; stocks then shift in the same direction.

If bonds have not yet broken down, this increases the stock market returns and maintains existing stock prices. The real risk starts to rise five to seven months after the bond market peaks or bottoms, followed by a six-month acceleration in stocks for path bonds.

Commodities and bonds usually have a reverse

relationship: with commodities increasing, bonds decline, but bonds rise as commodities decline. Expectations of inflation impact bond prices.

The movement of the US dollar related to shifts in monetary policy influences the price of commodities. Commodity bonds lead 12-18 months in advance (it takes longer to enforce the monetary policy) and 24-27 months before the economies completely adopt changes to policies.

Now, the relation between commodities and stocks

Stocks continue to be responsible for goods. Commodities cover inflation, with demand rises and higher inflation levels at the end of the business cycle.

Credit (loans) capital and business growth take time to work its way into the economic system, from price rises to rising inflation expectations. As a result, goods usually surpass at the end of the business cycle.

In general, increasing bond prices raise stock prices in recovery, with decreasing price of commodities attesting to the economic expansion. As expansion spreads and begins to decline, take note that bonds first decrease, followed by stocks (as interest rates rise).

After commodities overtake stocks and begin to turn down, it signals the end of the economic boom with the possible start of business weakening and then collapsing into an inevitable recession.

Retail traders will continue to learn about the economy through cross-market research and asset diversification. Nonetheless, they do not answer these key questions, but any retail asset allocation trading alternative with US$ 25-$50 K or less must tackle: how much capital is sufficient to adequately diversify risk apart from any asset class?

There was a mistake. if you can require diversification ...

How do you reconcile the several and continuously changing macro-economic ties with the exchange in the corresponding asset class?

Where can I learn how to use Intermarket research to profitably distribute retail assets? Follow the link below, entitled "Consistent Outcomes," to see the competitive portfolio of retail options traders between groups of assets to rotate in and out of inter-market ties.

How would it be?

The volatility of each asset class is exchanged through optional ETFs (Commodity, Emerging Market, Currency, and REIT) as well as optional broad / sector stock indexes. I don't have to explicitly exchange goods and currencies.

Note the addition/reduction of volatility within the portfolio, as not all Asset Groups, Sectors, or Individual Companies/ Countries simultaneously up / down ALL value; and/or all at the same rate.

CHAPTER 8

WEEKLY OPTIONS TRADING

Using weekly options, more safe traders are created by questions, emails, and forums "how and when to use" than by any other topic.

In this "chapter," we shall look at the possibilities and shortcomings associated with this interesting investment instrument more closely.

A look ahead: There are some strong conservative investor uses for weekly options, but they should be avoided for others because they offer a major profit to some types of investment situations. We will look at how, when, and why they suit your goals.

In 2005, fast analysis of weekly mechanic choices began, using the S&P 500 as the basis. Only in 2010 were weekly options available for individual stocks on different exchanges.

Daily options on several indices, ETF's and individual stocks are now open. The list is rising. (The list of traded "weeklies" is available separately from early 2012.)

Weekly options continue to trading on Thursdays and expire on Friday a week later (eight days). But they are not sold for the final week of normal monthly trading, because the prices of each week and month are the same in the final week before the expiry.

There are both "American style" and "EU style" options. American style can only be practiced on a day of expiration. As with daily monthly options, weekly options may be bought or sold before expiry.

The scarcity of weekly options is a big issue. Usually, the weekly volume of options is around 10% of the total underlying option value. The value is that smaller trading volumes are equal to wider bid spreads and, therefore, more slopping when joining or leaving a trade.

Time is of the essence

Not surprisingly, "time" is the key to ensuring that

weekly choices yield advantages over weeklies.

Weekly options are available in the setting where the time decreasing curve is steepest, i.e. when an option is decayed it is not standardized. Value erodes as soon as we expire.

The fact that the time value quickly decreases as an option hits the expiry is helpful if we purchase options weekly as the premium for extrinsic (time) is already steadily decreasing.

Inverse, option sellers (income seekers) do not earn a beneficial weekly premium unless they accept market strike rates. This question is compounded by the fact that stocks are shifting more and more every day.

In 2011, the overall value of S$ 500 swings by more than 2 percent every day on 15 percent of business days ... Compared to fewer than 9% of the previous year's days.

Daily options advantages

Decide when best-used In general, figures on buyers of options are very bleak. Many of the money options run out of favor, resulting in the loss of money for most outright traders in the long term.

There are, however, unique circumstances in which transactions can be viable.

Using Reverse Iron Condor weekly options makes sense as the premium is again slightly lower and there is less time to expire. (There is a separate White Paper on this technique.) You want to pay as little cost as possible, as it is a debit spread.

Cheap insurance related to a "case.

"Reports of earnings and other "documented" incidents can lead to significant price increases as they occur. Since time decline is eroding the value of options, a stock can be hedged (or a Monthly optional position of both types) at low premium costs with one weekly option, you can buy the weekly calls or puts for the week surrounding your planned announcement or event date.

When a betting game is pursued for the result of an event, i.e. a 'forward' trade, the weekly option preceding the event may give a lower premium cost than an earlier monthly or quarterly option. Again, that is because you're paying far less for it.

Iron Condor reverse.

Basically, this strategy consists of two spreads, such as an income-based Iron Condor, but spreads are "debit" spreads because you purchase near the strike price for each spread, and the shorter it is. The net difference for each Reverse Iron Condor spread is debited to your account rather than credited as for the normal Iron Condor charge.

Weekly Drawbacks

The drawback of weekly choices is basically corollary to their advantages.

Not favorable weekly choices for credit spread.

The fundamental premise of credit distribution strategy such as 'The Monthly Income Machine' is to provide a mechanism that can offer a substantial return with considerably less risk than other strategies for the conservative income-oriented investor.

Credit distribution income is based on earning benefit (premium), earned by purchasing speculators, by selling them the "money" they need to bet on their options.

Essentially, credit spread investors seek to receive the premium contained in the "time remaining for expiry" out-of-the-money option price. In the case of suitable base stock, ETFs and indices, the premium can be significant, even at striking rates, far from the current market.

Therefore, weekly options provide a lot less premium value for the seller of the right to order than he does by selling monthly options, because there is very little time in the life of the weekly right.

The only way to earn an enticing fee weekly is to shockingly close strike rates to the current market.

Many Possible Weekly Choices Sacrifices The Fun Aspect.

While the "action" given by weekly expirations allowing for further trading in the month could be doubtful to the thrill-seeker, it could be a potentially risky tentative for cautious investors to trading their accounts.

Commission costs.

Obviously, the passion of brokers for weekly options traders is overshadowed only by their passion of day traders. Although the costs of commissions in option-friendly brokers are now relatively normal, having 3-4 times as many businesses each month makes a small account very useful to the brokerage ... But for the trader not necessarily.

Wider spreads the bid-ask. As previously noted, weekly option volume and open interest were substantially lower than for monthly options. Consequently, when entering or closing a contract, you are likely to contend with a much greater price drop.

Theta risk

Theta, you may remember, is the indicator "Greek" that calculates the rate of decay of option value over time. The rate of loss of value of time decay accelerates explosively as options reach expiry.

With weekly options, when the place is set, a growing loss of value is already underway and accelerates every hour from that point. It is clearly at the expense of the choice investor.

Weekly choices are better used if we want to be in the game for a known case. The advantage of using weekly options rather than daily when purchasing puts or appeals is that there is less premium expense than months bought earlier; the option premium depends heavily on the amount of time remaining before expiry and the customers can pay the extra time.

From the point of view of premium stock, as with credit spreads, the reverse is the case. The monthly options offer a net seller option more premium than weekly-at the same price of the underlying stock, index, or ETF simply because the extra expiry period offers an additional premium value.

U.S. Government Warning Needed Commodity

Futures Trading Commission:

Trading futures and options have significant potential benefits, but also high potential risks. You must be mindful of the risks and be willing to embrace them to invest in the markets for future and options. You can't afford to lose with money.

It is not a proposition or an offer to buy/sell future or options. There is no indication that any account can or would possibly make gains or losses comparable to those mentioned on this website. Any trading system or methodologies past success does not automatically indicate potential results.

CHAPTER 9

TRADE PERFORMANCE METRICS

PORTFOLIO MEASURES

The profit gain and loss risk for retail option trading must be managed at two different performance levels: the portfolio and trade specifics.

At the portfolio point, there are three types of goals to be set even before you trade.

Minimum Return Objective:

Lowest measure acceptable, mostly possible, absent a disastrous market occurrence.

Using the historical S&P 500 annualized return as the lowest acceptable boundary between 10% and 12% (before the 2008 financial pandemic). S&P 500 is a commonly recognized index for trading stock, but the portfolio needs to be profitable-it doesn't count to be ahead of the $SPX on negative territory.

The T-Bill for 3 months, currently below zero, is below the historical annualized range of 10 percent to -12 percent. Although the T-Bill is a "completely" zero-risk investment, even the best investments bear a residual amount of risk irrespective of the minimal amount of risk. That's the case.

You have had all this Greek jargon and options not to make salads, but to resolve the share's success as an asset class.

If the return on your portfolio is almost zero and 10% -12% a year, you will delay reaching a point of pain which marks a failure to understand the ability of the baseline to manage risks. If your portfolio returns are between 0% and 12% and you intend to continue trading, processes will have to be re-engineered in your trade phase.

"Halt Trade" Objective: Accumulated losses hit an absolute value below the minimum return and must, therefore, be stopped entirely for a given time.

It is final to blow up your self-funded money. No

bailout package is available because a domestic options trading trade does not have access to bank loans or shareholders 'equity to fund their personal business.

Boiling down to trade output relevant indicators.

Characteristic features of a successfully controlled portfolio right before you measure the metrics are these: the largest loser doesn't exclude the largest winner. The biggest winner will be in many of the biggest losers, e.g. 2-3 times more.

Over and above the greatest losers, there are far more winners with higher income prices than the rising loser. Depending on the size of your account, the income will slowly increase.

In the tens of thousands, profits should grow steadily from the low hundreds to the lowest hundreds; from the higher hundreds then they will grow to the thousands.

If your account is over $100 K, income from hundreds to thousands will increase. Profits from low hundreds to thousands signal unsustainable dependency on gaping plays that can't help you steadily increase profitable performance.

What can I do about this portfolio behavior and trade efficiency indicators in a reliably competitive portfolio?

Check the portfolio of the trader model option which shows these characteristics.

Go to the difficult metrics. There are two ways to count your return on your commercial property.

The first way to take advantage of the trade account is to split the balance by the start of the year on 01/01/YYYYY.

The second approach is to divide the gross income of the trading account by the current net liquidating value.

In both cases, you can get a Total Net profit number minus the Total Profit Commission Expense. Then divide net income by the cash balance of the beginning of the year; or net liquidating value.

Net Cash Value is the amount of your complete

trading account that is equal to Total Cash + Stock Value + Product value + Bond value.

The beginning of the year cash balance is simple-it's the money on the account at the beginning of the financial year. When you have short securities, cash increases; so when you're long on securities, cash decreases.

Calculated these statistics using your income (wins) and losses (losers) from your account to test your performance: Win / Loss probability: is the number of wins divided by the total number of companies.

The other way to describe this win/loss ratio is to divide it by the number of losers.

The chance of win/loss; or, win by 1 loss, the ACCURATION steps in selecting businesses.

Average Win is equal to the sum of all profits divided by winning numbers.

The total loss equals the number of losers in all

defeats.

The average winnings separated by the average loss calculate if you RESPONSIVE gains and losses.

Combine the accuracy with the response ratio to achieve the output ratio.

Power Ratio = (Win / Loss Probability) x (Medium Win / Medium Loss). Aim always to keep the output ratio above 1.00.

Why?

The widely known money management rules should assign 2% -5% (60% x Net Account Value) per trade. The discipline of the reduction of + 1% in trade allocation between the 2%-5% allocation is not usual.

If you assign 2% per option trade, then you can raise it by + 1% to 3% if your return ratio is above 1.00 for the following month. Then, for every month you surpass 1,00, you will increase + 1 percent before you hit the upper limit of 5 percent.

If you assign 2% per option exchange, you will decrease it by -1% to 1% if you don't keep your output ratio above 1.00 for the next month. You will keep your trade allocation 1 percent for each subsequent month until you can set your output ratio above 1.00 to raise your trade allocation by + 1 percent again.

This is how the ladder effect is accomplished by rising profits and reducing losses. This up / down process is an important method for rewarding income and disciplining the risk of losses. You need both ACCURACY and RESPONSIVE before increasing the size of your position.

Where can I find out more about portfolio metrics as part of a complete trading system? Follow the link below and learn online options online from home for 55 hours.

People want to make money quickly. Options trading is the safest technique to use for that reason. When most people think about choices, they take a risky approach. They are really for those who don't trade them properly.

To order to build leverage and manage risk, stock options are used. The approaches I have learned from my mentors are effective and transparent when you hang them.

Two types of options, calls, and puts are open. There are two things you can do, buy or sell any choice. A protected call is the most common technique for using options. There are two different positions in the plan.

If you have long traded underlying xyz at $15.00 you can offer an option to call it and collect money on your account to offer it.

Buy 100 xyz shares for $15.00 and sell one contract (equivalent to 100 shares of shares) from 15 strike calls for 30 days before expiry and receive $1 per stock for a total of $100.

You get money at the expiration if xyz trades over $14.00. Sure, even though your stocks go down, you will make money!

- If XYZ is over 15 dollars, you sell your stock at 15 dollars and retain the 100 dollars you earn to sell the option at first.

- When you buy a call option, you are entitled to buy a certain underlying at a certain price for some time.

- If you sell a call option, you are obliged to charge a certain price for a certain amount of time.

- You have the right to sell a certain underlying at a certain price for a certain amount of time while purchasing a placement contract.

- If you sell an option, you have an obligation for some time to buy a particular underlying item at a certain amount.

If this is your first time I know it is difficult to learn about choices. But believe me, options trading will allow you to make money quickly.

By selling options, you can easily make money by generating a stable monthly income that can be regularly duplicated.

Making money in trade means giving yourself an advantage. You can do that exactly through sales strategies. 80% of options expire without interest! So who makes the most of the money? That's right, sellers pick.

Sale Choice

There are so many ways to make additional money. Options trading is the one that can change your life. There are so many cases in which you can choose to trade options that give you a statistical advantage.

Most people agree that options trading is dangerous. Most people risk money because of options trading! 80% of options expire without interest.

So, who makes all the money?

The people who purchase these products or who sell them.

The reason people say the choices are dangerous is that they don't. We would have a very different view if we did. Only ask a good supplier about what he or she thinks of choices. Market makers I follow know a lot about making extra money.

You'll tell a whole different story. When traded correctly, options rising risk and maximize benefit. I will show you some of my favorite tactics on this page that put me on the winning side. The hand I've got the math advantage.

Positive time decay means the prize decays or erodes every day that passes. In other words, if stock xyz trades $20 today and the $20 call trades $1.95, then a day later all other items are equivalent to $1.95 as there is less time to find it worth doing.

CHAPTER 10
VERTICAL SPREAD STRATEGY

In this chapter, I'm going to give you my plan and how to implement it for free. I heard this from many of my business mentors and many other things.

This is why I write this particular chapter; I love free money-making ideas. The strategy is not the answer. How I execute is the most important element. I'm going to show you both.

The technique is an alternative known as a vertical spread. Not fresh for someone who has previously traded options, but for those of you who haven't I'm going to first cover how I do it.

Here's an example of what I would do if I felt a stock I'd do the following.

- Xyz sold at $53.20
- sell xyz 55/60 for $2,00 for a credit 30 days until

expiry If xyz was going to increase I will do the following

- sell 50/45 for a credit of $2,00 for 30 days before expiry Let's use example # 2. The average benefit of this vertical distribution is $2.00. When you have not taken any action after you put the max loss of $5.00 (strike width) minus $2.00 (received credit) = $3.00.

I never take the full loss, however. The most I lose on this trade is half the full benefit, $1.00. I wouldn't do the trade if I couldn't get this amount.

I'd do that on a stock with a bullish pattern of candlesticks and put my stop order undercover. I'd sell the vertical spread above my stop loss.

The best thing about this trade is optimistic. In other words, all other things being the same, every day the vertical spread I sell becomes cheaper and cheaper as there is less time to end up ITM (in the money).

So, all I need is for xyz to stop trading and my spread is worthless. This is the best case.

The worst case is that I'm delayed. Less extensively evaluate all situations.

With xyz trading at $53.20, I'd probably stop at about $51.00. So I will win the trade if xyz never hits $51.00. If your technological know-how goes down, it will happen to you a lot of time.

If xyz, which was trading for $53.20 when I put the trade to $51.00, I would avoid the trade. My reasoning was incorrect and I lost the right to trade? Okay, it's up to it.

When I bring the contract on xyz trades down to $51.00 on the day I take $1.00 to the maximum loss. But what if I get stopped from now on for three days? Note that every day the choice I have sold is better and cheaper all other things are equal.

Trading these free money ideas means that the risk continues to decrease every day. Depending on a variety of different factors, what I noticed was if I sell a vertical spread with 30 days before expiry, like the above example, I would break even worse after about 15 days in the market if I get stopped.

That means, if xyz trades at $51.00 on the fifteenth

day, the price of my vertical spread will be the same as 15 days ago when stock trading was $53.20.

So why are these free money ideas made so good? Okay, if the stock increases, I make money if the stock is going sideways, I make the money when the stock falls and remains at $51.00. The only way I lose money is if the stock trades in the first 15 days are down to $51.00. So I make money if after fifteen days I get stopped.

Do you mean that I can be mistaken and still make money? Yup, this is a trade for those of us who know how to make use of options.

Oh yeah and all of that way, with this situation I make money over three out of four with a 2-1 risk-return ratio. That is, if I win, I'll do double what I lost if I stopped the first day.

The fact that the risk decreases day by day, as long as you are still in business, is the key part of this technique. The best thing about these free money ideas is that you can only lose $0.70 on the breadth if you get stopped on the 5th day.

When you can see with these free money concepts, the probability is for you. I must explain the key argument again to make this plan work.

- The only way to lose money is if you quit in the first 15 days. The amount you lose depends on how many days you spend before you quit.

- If you're not stopped, you're winning twice what you'd lose if you stopped on the first day.

- Over time, the cost of trade decreases and you will win over 50% of the time with a reward ratio of 2-1.

Note some of these key points in this approach.

1. I know what my average chance is

2. I've got a strategy for the entire trade

3. I have a risk/reward ratio of 2-1 4. My risk decreases every day, as I like free money making ideas, so I have written this post. This is a technique I encourage you to know because it works.

Technical research is the only other part you need to

understand to execute this strategy. You need to identify stocks that can be predicted through various approaches for technical research. Only make businesses that follow your guidelines and laws.

Efficient traders who regularly make money, regardless of the path the market goes, all share one thing. You know how to handle risk. They know how to cut short losses and make sales work.

They will thrive most importantly in the future trade as they have a successful trading strategy that gives them a new edge.

For example, if a trader is 40 percent correct, but he does twice as much on his winning trades as he loses on his losing trades. Is this trader going to make money?

Let's say he risks 200 dollars per exchange. In 100 companies, he will lose 60 and win 40. He would make 16,000 dollars on all his winners and lose 12,000 dollars on his losers for a net positive 4,000 dollars.

The purpose of this example is to illustrate why a plan is so necessary. If you want to make money quickly, you must manage the risk first. When you know how to enter and exit, which option or stock to buy, and how much to gamble per exchange, you can simply adjust your strategy which will be effective with time, as it has a mathematical edge!

CHAPTER 11

GETTING A TRADING EDGE IN OPTIONS TRADING

Most private traders claim that experts with strong analytical skills trade options. There are two reasons so many private traders think so. Too risky and complicated are options trading. Many private traders assume that trading stocks or futures is simpler.

So, a basic question is that it is so much simpler and less difficult to sell futures or to buy stocks, why are options available that can be traded?

The main explanation for this is that options, which vary from other trade instruments, can give private traders a trading advantage and allow them to flexibly cover almost every investment strategy and risk profile. In many respects, options are the best trading instruments currently used by many traders. You don't have to be a specialist in finance for trade options.

In Jack Schwager's book The New Business Wizards, he argues that no one can succeed without a break unless you have the world's highest discipline and financial management. If you are trading futures on the SPI, you must know exactly what your trading edge is, particularly if you are a professional floor trader.

You will be able to see with the trading edges the buy and sell orders leaving the trading pit and who is the buyer and seller.

Furthermore, the speed at which your orders are carried out and transaction costs should also be noticeable. The popularity of inventories, options, and futures is growing; so many people trade such goods. Just a limited number of these traders have a strong trade advantage.

The key reasons why many private traders in financial markets have struggled are lack of trading edge, weak risk management, and inadequate resources. The key point here is to find a new edge, make good use of it, and use effective risk and money management techniques.

If the odds are in your favor, you can learn how to trade. It is also necessary to ensure that you stand by if the odds are not in your favor. If you do, you have the greatest chance of success for yourself.

Trading networks have as many traders as they are. We're not going to trade a program if it doesn't give us an advantage.

When you have a program that can offer an advantage, why not improve the advantage in the right situation by options trading?

Before you put a trade, try to consider as many variables as possible in your favor. By doing this, you give yourself a much greater chance of long-term success.

There are no guarantees for any sort of trading. Compared to other people who know little about options and trade without a rim, you cannot help. Yet you have a great opportunity to fulfill your financial goals in the long term. Flexibilities provided by options are the following:

I) income generated from an upward or downward market correctly predicted.

ii) The future returns can be significantly increased with a fairly low payout.

iii) If the market is the way you intend, you have an infinite profit opportunity while restricting your risk by choosing an amount that you allow to risk.

iv) Income can still be achieved by carefully selecting where the market does not go.

(v) Benefit from the market of flat or non-trending phases.

vi) Income earned from time going from.

vii) Income earned at a rising pace as you continue to support the sector.

The alternative is an extremely versatile trading device. You can use options trading strategies that exactly suit your market views while closely sewing them to your specific risk tolerance level.

People who trade for a living and as their trade should seek to understand and apply the concepts outlined in this chapter. They do so because they know there is an edge to be gained in comparison to people who don't.

We are close to the traditional casino gambler if they do not trade with edge; their money will eventually be lost. You are just like the casino if you trade with the edge of trade. You probably have no chance to talk to those who trade in markets to make their living.

They look like an odd profession and these people are thought to be crazy mathematical geniuses who might give Kasparov their money to play at a chess tournament. The passion of traders for job opportunities does not go beyond truthfulness.

While many of the professionals involved in financial markets are smart people, they have not been in the genius category. However, they have one thing in common.

Throughout their options trading, they understood and applied those basic concepts. The concepts they used then offered an impetus for effective market trading. Therefore, they make a decent living in their options trading.

You don't need to be a trader of experienced options. The edge gave traders also to private traders from the values of skilled options. Practically, you can understand and apply these ideas and the results will help to push them more completely in your favor.

All the advantages that most traders with skilled options do not have. You can learn to make your trade more competitive by using the same concepts. You may also gain from a trading advantage in this way.

Find or build your own options trading scheme that is great stock options! This intelligent equity derivative must be one of the most brilliant inventions of modern times. There are many luxuries in life for the trader, who can know how to win on options trading.

Success in options trading needs a clear long-term

investment strategy. This statement is not meant for a grandiose, remark by some 'trading theorists,' but is rather a statement born of the author's tough knocks and achievements, as well as many other successful traders.

This 'consistent approach' to options trading can also be referred to as a 'trading scheme' or a 'trading system of options.' The term "trading device" is not inherently limited to a collection of computerized trading signals "black box."

A trading system may be something like "purchase an option on an upstream stock that breaks the high of the previous bar after at least 2 days of downstream movement to lower it." A trade system is essentially a structured strategy that profits from a repeated trend or occurrence that brings net benefits.

Since an option is a stock derivative, the trading strategy must come from a stock trading strategy. It means that the method will be focused on the real movement of stock prices.

That being said, the trading system does not have to operate with all inventories but only with certain stock types, certain stock volatility, and certain stock price rates, etc. ... So concentrate your trading program on those stocks that have a price history that is consistent with your net results.

You may establish a trading system, a trading strategy, and a trading technique by defining the pricing trend or any frequent event (or lack of a market movement trend). It means that you can swap market patterns in market diagrams like conventional diagrams, averages, swings, pivot points, frames, etc.

Or you can trade in stock price stimulating events such as income runs, post income runs, market splits, seasonal factors, and so on. In the final analysis, to make the most profit in the options trading, you want your stock to move quickly and push it further. Just a fairly low stock price change will double your cash options!

There are so many different variations and tactics

that you can exchange with options. Calls and directions can be purchased. You can use telephone calls and spreads in the direction of trade with buffered risk and benefit.

You can sell or lease expenses to earn premium decay credit by option expiry. You can swap straddles and strangles when you anticipate a great pass, but you are not sure where. You may also join, condors back spreads and butterflies in ratio ...

And if you feel nuts you should sell "naked" options (just use a stop loss or you'll end up like one of my old trading buddies who run an account at $20 million, then offer all of it back with naked options).

Trading networks for directional options are the best. Keep it easy, buy upside calls for trade or buy downside calls. However, this means that you need a directional stock trading program to trade directional options.

These are a few solutions to directional systems: build options trading systems that trade with the changes in stock price movement. Today, there are many successful swing trading schemes. We recommend that you get one.

Options Brokers now have advanced order technology to let you enter swing trading based on stock price movement so that you don't have to watch this market all day. This big step in swing options trading.

The majority of swing trading schemes are based on the stock price chart for daily bars.

Swing intra-day bars exchange!

Their other fantastic systems are based on diagrams that mark swing trade entries. Establish an options trading program that trades patterns for between three and six months. Here is the big money. Trading big developments is where others will invest more money to increase their net worth.

Build a trading framework for options trading pivot points. Pivot point trading is possibly the safest way to trade options, as price action is typically volatile and takes place rapidly on the way to sell. This is perfect because you can use shorter-term choices to make a little more use of yourself. And in five days to four weeks on average, it is also good to make major changes so that the problems of decline are less of a concern.

There are several different directional trading strategies for options trading. You need to pick one, work it, and never use more than ten percent of the place size for small accounts in big accounts. This way of handling money options trading is the quickest way to potentially quick account growth to avoid unnecessary backstops.

CHAPTER 12

EVALUATION OF VARIABLES IN OPTION PRICES

To quickly evaluate the variables in the option price, the option price will be determined by the price of the underlying security, by the strike price of the option, the time to expiration, the value of the underlying security, any outstanding dividends, and the present risk-free interest rate.

So why are seasoned traders worried about the "Greek Option?" It's because they are a valuable way to forecast what is going to happen to an option's price as market variables change.

This can seem at first difficult to understand, but the option prices do not necessarily change with the price of the underlying asset. Any trader who takes the time to learn the basics, however, will begin to understand the variables and the effect of each factor in moving the prices of an option.

Many business traders are using the Greek option to handle several multiple options effectively in a variety of strikes over many time frames. Market professionals will also use the Greeks to ensure that their risk exposure is efficiently hedged and adjusted accordingly, to build a balanced portfolio.

As far as the day trader or investor is concerned, the Greeks demonstrate how and why an option price changes when one of the variables changes.

The 5 options commonly listed in the Greek language are the delta, which calculates the connection between the price change option and the price change in the underlying stock.

Gamma-these tests the Delta's rate of transition

Vega, which measures the volatility change,

Theta-which measures the time shift, and

Rho, responsible for the interest rate shift

The Delta is the first and most frequently referred to

in Greek. As reported, the delta is the rate of variation in the option price relative to the underlying stock rate of change. This is crucial to understand because many of our option strategies are designed to take advantage of a strong prediction of the underlying security price shift

For an example of Delta, we have a $50.00 stock and a $50.00 cash flow option. There are 30 days before expiry; the call option is $2.32 and the Delta 0.53. The delta represents the predicted change, given that there are no other variables.

If the stock price rises to $51.00 by one dollar, we should assume that the call option will rise from $2.32 to about $2.85.

Likewise, if the stock price drops down from $50.00 to $49.00, we would expect the call option to decrease in value to approximately $1.79 from $2.32.

Note that the price has changed by the sum of the Delta in both cases. Several of the Delta's main characteristics are: When a call option becomes broader, the delta reaches 1.

There is always a favorable delta for call options.

At the point where this option delta hits 1, the call option will represent approximately the dollar's price movement of the underlying stock.

If we look at the delta of a put-on option, the larger the option is, the delta is less than 1. Put options should have a negative delta always.

The next Greek choice is Gamma.

Since the delta is always rising, this radical shift had to be calculated. As a result, the Gamma was created to measure the rate of delta transition. This is mostly used by practitioners to change the hedged portfolios of the Delta.

Vega is the next Greek Option.

Vega is the calculation of the variance of the option price in relation to the increase in implied volatility percentage. For this example of Vega, there is an inventory at $50.00 and an alternative at $50.00. There are 30 days before the expiry. The call rate is $2.06 with a 35% Implicated Variance and a corresponding Vega of 0.057.

If the implied stock volatility increased by 1% to 36%, the call option will increase from $2,06 to approximately $2,12 the Vega price.

In the same way, if the implied volatility drops from 35 percent to 34 percent, we would expect to decrease the value of the call option from $2.06 to about $2.00.

The next Greek choice is Theta.

The Theta is a function of the price shift relative to the time change to maturity. A choice loses some value every day that passes, the Theta calculates the decay rate.

For this example, we have a $50.00 stock with the $50.00 cash option and a $50.00 cash option. There are 30 days before the expiry. The call is priced at $2.06 for a Theta of less than 0.041. If the number of days before expiry dropped from 30 to 29 days, the Theta option will decrease from $2.06 to around $2.02.

Greek's final choice is Rho.

Rho is a calculation of the increase in the option's price relative to the increase in the risk-free interest rate. This particular Greek is much more important in terms of long-term choices as the short-term interest rate effect is less evident.

For this example of Rho, we have a stock that costs $50.00 and an option for $50.00. There are 30 days before the expiry. The call option is $2.06, with interest rates at 3.00% and a Rho of 0.02.

If interest rates rose to 4 percent, the option price would rise from $2.06 to $2.08, Rho's value, while the option price would decline from 3 percent to 2 percent, from $2.06 to $2.04.

In conclusion, an investor or trader will understand by studying the Greek option why the option is or isn't linked to the underlying security.

Through knowing certain factors influencing option prices, regular traders or investors have the confidence to incorporate options into their portfolios and use various approaches to help them achieve their goals.

CHAPTER 13

ANALYZING MARKET TRENDS IN OPTIONS TRADING

Nearly every option trader has heard the old trade adage that says, "The trend is your buddy." In reality, an option trading against the current market trend certainly puts the odds of winning for you. So many newcomers have lost whole accounts through the purchasing of call options from the bear trend market and the purchasing of options from the bull trend market.

Yeah, what is a business phenomenon exactly?

Trends in the market are like ocean tides. You know that it's a rising tide when you see the sea rise higher and higher and when you see the beach more and more, you know that it is an ebbing tide.

Similarly, you know it's a bullish phenomenon when you see the bigger and higher indexes like the Dow

Jones Industrial Average or the S&P500, and you realize it's a weird phenomenon when you see the smaller and lower indexes.

Yeah, market patterns are general movements that tend to shift stocks. During a bull market, the prices of most stocks will rise and grow, and the prices of most stocks will decline and drop.

One thing about trends is, however, that trends are a "general course of movement". It does not mean that a bull trend just drives the market up every day and does not mean that a bear trend just drives the market down.

When you watch the ocean tides, the water does not rush on the beach in a rising tide but falls in the waves. One wave is stronger than the last. The same is true of stock market patterns. You will see days interspersed with days in a bull cycle. However, notifications will occur more regularly and will every after each slight retreat.

This also shocks new traders who view the first day

in a bull trend as the "birthday" market. That is how both newcomers and experienced traders in options fall into the proverbial "Bull Trap" and "Bear Trap," which are brief counter-trend shifts that are misinterpreted as trend adjustments.

Traders who fall for either trap are usually shocked when the general trend resumes and are stuck in a losing position which never turns around.

Recognizing how patterns work is just the first step to business patterns identification. Have you ever believed that the economy is just one way to disagree with it by peers? How can two people who look at the same market draw different conclusions about the trend in the market?

The challenge of understanding consumer patterns is that the demand can be in all three directions at any point on the same day!

The market might be in a downturn for day traders, but on the same day, it could be in a bull downturn for a day trader and a long-term investor's neutral pattern.

How can that be?

In reality, there are not just "business" conditions; depending on the timeframe, there are multiple market conditions! It is not known that there is a common consumer trend for various trade horizons and investment targets, which contributed to all the pointless debates about what the business trend is in television.

If you have a charting program you may get surprised to watch it sometimes. Depending on your timeline, 1 min chart, daily chart, weekly chart, or monthly chart, you might find a completely different chart pattern on the same index.

A diagram that looks incredibly strange in the 1-minute table might look extremely stable and chaotic on a regular map. As such, trend analysis includes in the first place an appreciation of the exact time frame in which you trade.

Acknowledgment of the exact time you are trading is an extremely important precondition for options trading, where the contracts and positions you have bought are time-sensitive! Yeah, options do not last forever, and all choice approaches have an optimized return period.

For example, the market trend you would be concerned with will be the intraday trend most widely associated with minute charts, whether you are trading on the day with options and either writing or purchasing the options to close them for profit by the end of the trading day.

In this situation, whether the market is in a long-term bull or bear trend no longer affects your trading. The world may be crying, but if your minute charts show bearish for the day, the way you make your money is bearish.

If you trade a covered call, you will want to write the call options on a stock that is fairly lateral to the market trading charts in the regular charts if you want to prevent the allocation of stocks.

In comparison, if you buy long-term LEAPS options,

you may be more interested in what the long-term market trend is instead of being too concerned with uncertainty every day.

So, what are the most important methods for identifying business trends?

Most veterans can identify the pattern in which a map looks much like a price chart. However, countless complex technological metrics have been developed over the years for the less skilled or technically inclined.

Personally, the Simple Moving Average is the most tested. That simply averages the price over a period of time to see where it normally goes. This is what I focus on most of the time personally and I use a different average period for different time horizons. The 30days or 50days are most widely used.

CHAPTER 14

THE BASICS OF TRADING STOCK OPTIONS

The equity option is a legal contract where the investor is entitled to purchase or sell 100 shares of equity of the firm (the strike prices) for the duration of the contract at a pre-determined price. A call option is a 100 share buy contract, and a put option is a 100-share selling contract.

In general, the person who sells the device can sell it because he pays a premium in return for losing his 100 shares. Both put-in and call plans are given up to three years in advance with specific expiration dates.

The longer the option remains, the higher the premium the call writer will charge. The most important thing to remember about options is that they expire after a certain period of time, unlike the stock at the base (option contracts will last from one week to three years).

The investor is prepared to pay the premium for the right to hold the stock in the future when he or she buys temporary leverages. Leverage in the sense that the returns will be fantastic, but time-limited, whether the stock moves dramatically up or down so that options will expire without interest if the stock price doesn't move up or down as the investor expects.

Federal and state legislation allows brokerage companies to ensure that clients are aware of the risks and are properly qualified and solvent for commercial options.

Various brokers have very different criteria, and sometimes these conditions are changed because of changes in the current economic environment, but some stock trading experience is required in all cases.

Brokerages typically sell a total of three rates of options trading. The first stage is the selling of "closed" options per stock you own already, i.e. the selling of closed calls.

The second level consists of acquiring and putting

options as either portfolios or hedges and the third level is cleared for the selling of options even though you don't own the 100 shares that underlie each contract you sell. It is called "naked" calling or placing choices.

Selling covered calls

The following is an example of selling covered calls. If an investor has 10,000 A shares, he or she can sell up to 100 covered calls or calls based on such shares. Most investors who sell or place covered calls use a revenue strategy.

They expect to collect the premium from the sale of the options and hold the stock after the expiry date of the option agreements. Selling covered calls is a perfect, fairly conservative strategy if you have a stock you are confident would not go up before the sales expire.

If your inventory has just an income report and no information is anticipated for a while, why not sell calls and make a couple of bucks of premiums while you wait.

However, if fantastic news arrives and the inventory price increases above the strike price of the call you sold, the stock will be called off and the new owner will earn some value above the strike price. You get the strike price per share, of course, and you don't lose money, just don't make the profit you would have on the stock if you haven't sold the covered calls.

Investors buy bills and calls usually purchase bills and calls as leveraged investments or as hedges for investment already available (think insurance).

There are several buying strategies to optimize your investment returns such as bolts, strangles, and so forth (to be discussed briefly below), but the basic approach is to use a call or put as an investment tool for a "long" or "short" investment that is time-limited.

Another simple approach is very close to the concept of insurance when buying outs or calls. If you already have 10 000 shares in a small biotech trade that has a big FDA approval decision, you might consider purchasing a few sticks with rates lower than the current stock price as an 'insurance' to cover yourself if the FDA fails to grant you an endorsement (putting up substantial sums of value with a significant stock price fall)

This is highly speculative where the investor does not own the underlying stock. It is necessary to note that with each option contract, the buyer is liable to buy 100 shareholdings from the underlying equity if / when the purchasers wish to follow the option contracts.

If all goes as expected, you get the refund for the optional contracts you have been selling without having to buy shares, but if things are going against you, you have to buy 100 shares for each contract you have sold that is being exercised.

This can lead to major losses, and brokers ensure that they know that you have sufficient assets to cover possible losses until it allows them to participate in the selling of naked puts and calls advanced option strategies.

The basic concept behind designing an option is to pre-define the risk while making the best use of the options to increase the future income.

Added spreads are designed to benefit from stock volatility or lack of stock volatility. Some spread strategies such as bull spreading or bear spreading are conceived to be profitable if stock prices are expected to shift moderately, whereas other strategies such as the spread of Iron Condor are established for benefit even if the stock is being exchanged in a narrow range.

The spreads of options can be very simple, such as bull call spreads involving a long leg or a short leg or quite complex butterfly spreads involving many calling and positions.

CHAPTER 15

UNDERSTANDING STOCK OPTION CONTRACTS

The stock options contract is one of the most popular terms misunderstood in the world of options trading.

What is a stock option contract exactly?

While at first glance it may seem overwhelming, it's much simpler than it was. Let us first start with a very simple description of what an option is: a buyer has the right to purchase or sell the underlying goods at a certain price by a certain date in the future, but not the obligation.

This is precisely the alternative-the alternative of being long or short in the future at a certain date. This form of contract is often based on a bond or shares underlying it. In the case of stock, a contract is equal to 100 stock shares. In the future, it would be equal to one underlying contract.

The so-called Strike Prices options often require a special price, known as a strike or striking price. This strike price is the price at which the underlying contract may be purchased or sold.

The strike price is also called the exercise price. Any of the underlying trades would have higher costs than others. For example, unfriendly stocks may have shocking price increases of $2.50 while the more reasonably priced stocks can have increases of $5.00 with much more expensive stocks.

Let's take an example:

Suppose an investor has shares of XYZ traded at 25 dollars a share.

Suppose that the investor expects that the shares will rise soon but does not commit the capital required to purchase the shares in full.

Instead, the investor can choose to purchase a call option. In this particular case, the investor may opt to buy a call of $27.50 in the first month. This call option will give the buyer the right to buy the options or the options at any time from $27.50 before they expire.

Suppose that after the investor has bought this call contract the shares will rise to $30 per share. If the investor has the right to a limit of $27.50 the investor will be aiming for a $2.50 share benefit minus any premium he or she paid on the call.

It is really important to understand fully how these contracts work before looking at their use.

Options also have an expiry date

When an option is listed, the expiry date is always present.

These days there are several different forms of expiry dates and more will certainly be added in the future. Different inventories and goods can also have specific expiry dates.

For instance, most highly traded stocks have options that expire every month. Such options expire every month on the third Friday. Some stocks will also contain end-of-month options and weekly options.

It's because every choice has a short lifespan.

Due to the fact the options have a short lifetime, a time decline commonly known as theta decline may occur throughout its existence. Theta is one of the most popular Greek choices and must be well known to use them.

Why do options have an expiry date?

Okay, a leveraged transfer of risk is one way to look at an option contract. The concept of a choice contract is in many ways identical to an insurance policy.

When an insurance policy is bought, a time period is also added to it. Every year, many policies must be updated. You pay the insurance provider a fee over the contract term to bear the risk of failure over that time. The insurance provider can no longer bear the risk after the contract ends unless the policy has been extended and a further premium is paid.

Options are somewhat similar as the issuer of an option bears the risk of making a particular move by a stock or the underlying contract. Like the insurance firm, the contract seller is paying a premium. However, once this option expires, the option seller no longer assumes the risk.

Options may be in, out, or at-the-Money Contracts through be in-money, out-of-money, or out-of-money when looking at options.

An option with the money is an option whose strike price is higher or lower than the actual underlying price. For example, if JJJ's stocks are trading at $50 per share and one has a call of $45, the call option is considered in money since it is above the strike price. This option is considered in money.

Using the same example, if you hold the $50 call option, that option will be valued based on the sum since the underlying shares are currently trading at that price.

Finally, the $55 call option is deemed to be out of the money if the underlying shares do not meet or surpass the impact price of $55.

The value of an option is known as the premium

when selling options, an option is known as the default value. This premium is the price at which the right can be bought or sold.

In certain words, if an investor decides to purchase but not to buy or sell the stock at any price in the future at a certain date, he or she will pay the seller of the option a premium. If the option is available, the seller retains the premium.

Available premiums can be relatively narrow or fairly wide. These are frequently quoted by market makers whose job is to make this alternative a market.

Market makers tend to take advantage of the opportunity to purchase the trade and sell it. However, the investment public has no such ability, so it is likely that if options trading buys the trade or sells the bid or even trade between these rates.

Options for smaller premiums, such as less than $3.00, are often offered in increments of $.05 whereas options for larger premiums are priced at increments of $.10.

There are two types of choice interest contracts consisting of two types of interest known as intrinsic and foreign.

The intrinsic value is the value of the option that is in the money while the extrinsic value is derived from the time value of the option.

The options can consist of both value types or consist entirely of one or the other at the same time.

For example, an out-of-money option is entirely foreign or time, whereas a deep in-money option is almost entirely intrinsic.

Eligible options Contracts can be purchased, sold, or purchased and sold in different combinations.

There are two types of choice contracts known as a call and a put option.

Using these two different kinds of contracts, several optional strategies can be created and used to try to hedge current positions, to make a steering wage on stocks or markets, and to benefit from time decline.

One of our favorite strategies is to use an alternative income strategy that can deliver a very low-risk approach for producing reliable market income with very little maintenance and a very high likelihood of success.

CHAPTER 16

ADVANTAGES OF TRADING SCHEME LEVERAGE OPTIONS

At its heart, a trading scheme of options is a mechanism for the creation and selling of signals using a validated stock analysis tool.

The program can be based on some kind of alternative approach and includes both basic and technical evaluations. Options trading systems may concentrate on changes in the underlying stock price, interest, decay time, unusual purchasing/selling behavior, or a mix.

Essentially, it is a checklist of conditions that must be met before entering trade. When all conditions are fulfilled, a signal is produced to buy or sell. The criteria for each type of option trading strategy are different.

Whether it's lengthy calls, covered calls, bear spreads, or naked index options, each one has its own type of a trading system. An optional salt trading program can help you get out false signals and create trust in entries and exits.

How relevant is a trading network for options?

The demand for options is very complex. Trading without a framework is like building a house without a plan. Movements of price, time, and stock will all impact your earnings. You must be mindful of each of these variables. Emotion can easily be swayed as the market shifts.

With a program, the response to these natural and usual emotions can be controlled. How much did you sit and watch a trade losing money when your order was filled?

Or, have you ever seen a stock price spike when you think of buying it? It is important to have a clear strategy in place to make rational and reasonable trade decisions. You can boost your trade executions by designing and following a good program, as emotionless and automatic as a machine.

Advantages of Trading Scheme Leverage Options

– Selling options have stock market leverage. You can control hundreds or thousands of shares with options at a fraction of the stock price itself.

A change in stock values from five to ten percent may be equivalent to an increase of one hundred percent or more. Seek to focus on percentage gains against dollar losses in your exchange. It needs a radical shift in traditional thinking, but it is necessary for the effective management of the trading system.

Objectivity – A successful trading scheme of options is focused on observable parameters that allow signals to be bought and sold. It takes subjectivity and second-guessing out of your business so that you can focus on predetermined variables that trigger explosive trade.

Flexibility – Almost all options traders can tell you that options give your trading flexibility. The demand for options makes it remarkably easy to take advantage of short-term positions.

You may build strategies for overnight gains with clearly specified risk with earnings events and weekly options. There are many ways to benefit from the trend to the range of any kind of market situation.

Security-The options trading program will serve as a hedge against certain investments, depending on an acceptable strategy in prevailing market conditions. This is a way of using defensive puts.

Risk – The trading structure of good options reduces the risk in two essential ways. Cost is the first method. The option prices are very small relative to the same quantity of inventory. The second way issues end. A successful system will easily reduce losses and keep them low.

The more tools in your toolbox, the more able you are to adjust business conditions. Unless the markets were to act in the same way every day, trading would become a play for children. To start designing your options trading, you have to build a trading strategy or strategy to lead you in the right direction.

Start with the basic framework and tweak it to identify and enhance your trading criteria. It takes time and experience to develop a productive options trading program that can return 100 percent or more in consistently profitable businesses. If you are pleased with your machine parameters, you can look at the automatic trading of your program.

CHAPTER 17

CHOOSING THE RIGHT OPTIONS BROKERS

Before I launch into the various requirements to determine prospective options brokers, I want to lay the groundwork by defining the world of successful options traders. My country, at least. I think you can see why I have the requirements I have to do.

The world of the active trader of options

I say I am an active trader of options, I mean that I frequently enter options trades in various ways. I also say I can do this many times a day. I agree to enter a trade, evaluate quickly and I would like to set up the trade and pick and enter a price and quantity. Often the market moves so quickly that the window of opportunity is a matter of minutes.

Often I have the same necessity to leave or change trade. I want the opportunity not only to position orders quickly but also to create standing orders quickly that will help me get out of business when I have a target profit point or I have reached my maximum allowable point.

Due to the nature of my trade, I rely on the trade having some theoretical edge. So I can sell a spread for more than the price and buy a spread for less than the price of the order. I always seek to hit the midway price between the bid and the demand level. As a consequence, I need to obtain the best possible price on either side of the trade.

Another critical aspect of my trading is the ability to determine rapidly my overall positions as a portfolio and know where I am in my overall exposure to the delta and the other Greeks. Good trading for me requires management of my portfolio and overall management risk, so I need to get a fast view of these values.

The last part of my life I want to cover is to be smooth. During my business, I often ask questions that I want to answer quickly. Some of these include:

How much credit will I get for this position?

What can I do to close my position?

If I add to my position, how does my overall portfolio influence?

What is the best way to cover some of my risk?

In this context, I want to turn now to the three main criteria, which I find relevant when evaluating options brokers.

Criteria # 1: trading platform

I stated earlier that for me as an active trader of options, agility is critical. To me, the trading platform is a gateway to agility. It is vital that questions can be answered quickly, evaluated, a hypothetical trade defined and various parameters modified before placing an order.

To do all this I also have to access information such as P&L maps, risk profiles, potential theoretical stocks,

stocks, and volatility, etc. I sometimes turn back and forth between the various areas of knowledge. I need a forum to keep my order information pending while I study more.

I will need a forum to answer all my questions quickly. When I think of credit or a calendar spread, I want to know what the credit might be quick. I want to know the delta, theoretical size, probability of the expiry of the short strike, etc. Might I want to know the possible extent of the underlying stock or ETF movement over a defined time frame?

Charting is important, of course, and almost all trading platforms have some sort of charting tool. I consider the ability to analyze, to see various time frames, and to annotate a diagram to be important.

Criteria # 2: Order routing

I said that I must have a good theoretical edge. I will say that the best theoretical advantage for a broker is worth the incremental fee it may cost for trade. The ability to obtain good fill prices is usually related to order routing (provided there is ample open interest).

For me, the routing of orders has two aspects. Firstly, my order is sent to the largest variety of exchanges of options. Many trade options on more than one exchange and therefore contribute more to equal trading and a more liquid market.

The second factor is the pace of the exchange of my order. I want my order in the perfect world when I click the send button. Time is important with rapid price movement.

Criteria # 3: Support and education

While a little less crucial than the first two criteria, I still regard support and education as extremely significant. There were several occasions when I looked at a position and suggested an improvement and I just wanted to get an opinion on my research (Note: I don't ask 'I should make the trade?').

There is nothing to say if I forget anything in my study like being on the phone or a conversation with somebody at the brokerage. It's a big help to have people who are active traders too because they speak my language and understand my culture.

Any options that offer ongoing, high-quality education would support both traders and brokers. The stronger I become, the more time I spend in the business, the more I trade, the more commissions they earn.

I have an interest in an option trader who is willing to invest in a range of education programs designed to improve me as a trader and potentially my trade.

Why are commission rates for brokers not on my appraisal requirements list?

The commission rates have been substantially reduced these days. In addition, it is always difficult to make true comparisons between apples. For me, the advantages of choosing a brokerage that meets my other three requirements far outweigh the extra $.50 or $1 I pay for a transaction per contract. Don't be drawn in by seemingly small fees on options trading.

CHAPTER 18

PREMIUM SELLING FOR LOW MAINTENANCE OPTIONS TRADING

I admit that. I love opportunities that include being a net premium seller. This method gives me less time to do transactions, more space for a mistaken course, and, best of all, I don't need a big business account.

I want to speak in this chapter about some of my favorite premium-selling tactics and include some quick tips on how to sell them for minimal investment time.

Summary of the option spreads

Before I start to address the strategies, let me provide a brief overview. The basic concept of a spread is to buy one option and to sell another. This typically has the benefit of creating a fixed risk role, but it essentially gives up the limitless profitability of purchasing an option.

My favorite strategy is a short, vertical spread, where I sell an option near the actual trading price, and buy a strike price further from the current price than the strike I sold.

This business is paid and the risk is limited to the dollar difference between long and short strike rates less the credit that I got. The greatest advantage in this trade is the credit I get from the selling of the spread. I will be able to maintain this credit when the short strike expires by $0.01 or more from the money.

Why is this my favorite approach?

Let me demonstrate with an illustration. Let's say that SPY, currently trading at $108, was in a bullish tendency late, and my prediction (20-40 days) was that SPY would drop sooner or later.

A vertical spread trading I could do is sell a SPY option at 104 $for a month, with 20-40 days until the end and buy a 102 $option. That is a large spread of $2 and can be put on for $0.50, so my exchange risk is $1.50. It will cost me $200 for one trade, and my overall risk will be $150.

When the trade begins, what are the opportunities? SPY will push strongly and I will close the trade within a week for a $.10 debit locking in $.40, a 26% ROI. However, for the next month, SPY could go sideways or even pull back a few dollars.

My trade still makes money in all these situations. Why is it?

Since I offered a 100% time premium with no intrinsic value out of the money option. In such a situation, time is my mate. Though I have a long-established option which is also wasting off, the value was initially lower so if both expire worthlessly, I end up with a net credit.

Creation of a trading plan

To simply know about the strategy is not necessary. To succeed in the long run, I need to follow clear rules which dictate when to get into a trade, when to get out of it and how much risk to take on the trade. These principles are a central part of a trading option strategy.

I've got one for this plan, which I will explain briefly.

I sell short verticals both bullish and bearish. For this topic, I'm just thinking about bullish trade and I'm leaving the bearish for the listener.

Outlook: Trading this strategy on the backdrop (normally an ETF) with a steady bumpy pattern (higher and higher lows) entrance: Look for an option with the remaining 20-40 days before the end and I seek to sell a few money strikes at short distance.

I often prefer $2, because Exit is easy to handle the margin requirements and risk: I have at least one trade profit goal and a "worst-case" scenario described as exits. One easy thing for me is what I call the 20%/100% law.

I will quit when only 20 percent of the initial credit remains in the trade. I will also leave if the cost of closing has risen by 100%. For instance, if I trade $.50, then my best exit is to close for $.10 (rule of 20 percent), while my 'worst-fall' exit is $1.00 (rule of 100 percent).

Obviously, this is a very simple trading strategy that needs to be established, which provides a very low maintenance approach to option trading. I may enter my exit rules as a 'one-cancel-other' order with several trading platforms, in which all orders are entered and if you activate one, the other one is canceled. That's it – it doesn't have to, no noise.

Another tactic that I like when I am neutral is what is called an iron condor. This is when I offer both a short vertical call and a short vertical call for the same month. I typically have at least $4 between the short and the short call with a $2 widespread. Thus, in the SPY position I listed, the call could spread over $114/112 and spread over $104/102.

The advantage of this approach is that it earns the same risk premium twice. Think about it. Think about it. Is it possible for SPY to be above $110 AND below $104 after expiration? No. No. Many brokerages would therefore only have a margin for this kind of trade on one hand.

Another technique I like is the distribution of the calendar. I may buy a $104 put on SPY for a couple of months then sell a $104 put off 20-40 days before expiry. In addition, this is a debit distribution but still a premium sales strategy. It's a little longer-term plan, but it can pay pretty well.

CHAPTER 19

OPTIONS FOR FLEXIBLE INSTRUMENTS

This chapter discusses which options and explains some of the options traders can use with these flexible instruments.

Options provide the buyer with the right to purchase (a call option) or to sell (a put option) the underlying stock or future contract at a specified price up to a defined date, but not with the obligation.

In other words, options are like contracts for tradable insurance.

An investor can purchase a Put option as a hedge against a stock price drop or a call option if the stock increases. The buyer has time to determine whether to purchase or sell the underlying stock by buying an option. The price is locked up until the expiry date, which could be years in the future for LEAPS.

Options trading has many benefits, such as high

leverage, lower average risk than owning physical assets, improved flexibility, and the potential to produce extra earnings from the current stock portfolio.

The value of an option fluctuates directly with the underlying security. The option price is just a small part of the security price and thus brings high leverage and lower risk – the most option holder can lose is the premium or deposit charged upon entering into the contract.

A much bigger loss is likely when the price goes against the buyer's position by acquiring the underlying stock of futures itself.

An option is indicated by its symbol, whether it is a call or a put, a month of expiration and a strike price.

A call option is a bullish contract that grants the buyer the right, but not the obligation, to purchase the underlying security, at or before a certain date.

A Put option is a bearish contract that gives the buyer the right but not the obligation to sell the underlying security on or before a certain date at a certain price.

The expiry month is the month in which the term for options expires.

The striking price is the price the buyer may either purchase a call or sell (put) the underlying security by the date of expiry.

The premium is the cost of the product.

The intrinsic value is the difference between the actual security price and the option's effect price.

The time value is the difference between the option's present premium and the intrinsic value. The stability of the underlying security is also affected by the time value.

Up to 90% of all cash options vest without interest and their period interest slowly decreases before the expiry date.

This hint provides traders with a very clear idea of which side of a contract for options they will be ... skilled traders who make regular profits usually sell far more options than they buy.

The options they purchase are usually to hedge only their actual stock portfolios-it is a powerful distinction between the punters and the small traders, who regularly buy low costs, capital and calls close to their expiry in the hope of a big pay-off (unlikely) and the guys who make money from the market options every month by actively selling these things.

If the buyer wants to exercise the right, the seller of the right contract must comply.

Therefore, if the stock price is higher than the option price at expiry, the option is said to be in-the-money, and the seller must market his shares to the option purchaser at a strike price, if exercised.

Often an option in the money is not exercised, this is very rare. The option seller (or author) must be ready to sell the stock, if exercised, at the strike price.

He can also buy back the option before expiry if he wants to write one at a higher impact price if the stock price has recovered, but this leads to a capital loss because he is usually responsible for paying more back than the premium he earned after the initial selling of the option.

Many option writers are simply exercised out of the stock, buy more of the same or another stock immediately, and simply write more calling options.

The holder of an option has no commitments at all – either he eventually sells his option for a profit or a loss, or he does so because his Stock price expires, and he will make a profit.

The vast majority of options are kept before they expire, and the price is decayed until the poor investor has no point in selling them. The buyer exercises very few options. The vast majority is useless.

All this being said, let us look at an example of how options can be used to obtain leverage in stock pricing when the trend favors us.

We will use MSFT as the underlying protection for this example. Suppose MSFT is trading a share of

$24.50 and this is early January. We are positive on this stock and we assume it will be $27.50 in a two-month timeframe based on our technical analysis.

In this example, we ignore brokerage costs, but they influence percentage returns. The prices and market changes of the stock and the options are hypothetical – only a guide is intended.

Buying 1000 physical shares will cost $24,500 and, when we sell our stake at $27.50 a share, our return on our money will be $3,000 or 12%. We are at risk of $24,500 if we take this position for a benefit opportunity of 12 percent or $3,000.

Rather than use cash to purchase the physical stock, we could purchase ten calling options, with an expiry of at least three months and a strike price similar to the current security price.

The call option is bullish, 3 months before expiry gives us enough time to turn quickly and the buying of an option at a price similar to MSFT's current price helps us to gain the full potential of the intrinsic benefit.

We buy 10 April Call options for MSFT $22.50. These options are currently available for $2.80 and are in the pocket.

$24.50 (current stock value of $22.50, minus $22.50, which is our intrinsic value) is $2.00. The Intrinsic value $2.80 (option premium) minus $2.00 gives us the Time value of $0.80.

If rates hit $27.50, as we assume they will, then the intrinsic value of the same options is $5.00 ($27.50 − $22.50). This means that if the Stock earns a share of $27.50, our compensation will be at least $5.00 plus a reasonable period depending on the time left before it expires.

Ten contract options would cost us $2,800 ($280 by 100), so if MSFT's value goes to $27,500, we can pay at least $5,000 ($500 by 10) for our choice contracts, maybe more.

We are at risk of $2,800 if we take this position rather than the full stock price ($24,500), for a possible benefit of 80 percent or $2,200 plus any remaining time value, potentially a further $100.

Our strategy for purchasing options gave us a far greater percentage profit with a much smaller risk. Do not forget, however, that these options for us as consumers will expire worthless unless sold or exercised by the expiry date.

The seller or writer will simply sit back and wait until the end to see whether he will be exercised. When the stock price is below the strike price, the premium is held, and an option can be entered on the same stock.

If the stock price is higher than the strike price, it is most probably exercised and will sell its shares if the stock price does not leave its position by purchasing its options back on the open market.

The downside to purchasing the option over the actual stock was that if you purchased the stock itself, even though the rates had not risen, you will still own it, but if you purchase the option, you lose part of your trading capital if the price does not shift in the desired direction.

To make options trading work, the underlying security must shift very rapidly in the direction you intend or, with the expiry date approaching, you lose money at an ever-growing pace.

As you can see, option strategies can offer much higher yields with a lower risk to the same trade. The bulk of your cash is not exposed to the market but still secure in your trading account.

This is just one example of how to increase the stock market returns with options trading. There are several more approaches and ways of using choices and I encourage you to further explore them.

Both options expire without interest unless they are in the money at expiration, so the investor needs to close or exercise his place before or on expiry, otherwise, he will lose the maximum premium.

The time portion of the option premium slowly

declines until the expiry date. The closer it expires, the sooner the time value will be decreased as there will be less time for the customer to travel in the desired direction.

For purchasers, the top traders suggest that they never have an option less than 30 days to expire as the time of decline rises exponentially.

The buyer of these options has the odds against them, which would entail a big price shift in his desired direction, to make profit-note, the overwhelming majority of the options are worthless-and that's the side of those instruments which are generally rich

For sellers, it is typically most lucrative to write options with 30 days or less to expire because of the time decay.

CHAPTER 20

OPTIONS TRADING USING ARBITRAGE

People still wonder if there is a way you can invest risk-free in the stock market. Are you 100 percent sure that you can make a profit once you get into your position?

The reply is 'yes.'

I will explain in this chapter how this technique works but have to preface our comments by saying that we believe that you understand how inventory solutions work and, in particular, concepts like income, income, etc.

'Time decay' 'strike price' 'Expiration assignment' and 'Expiration date.' If you are a little more experienced and know the definition of 'implied volatility,' it will be a bonus but not a necessary one.

If you don't understand the above definitions, you have to first read the basics, then come back and see this.

How organized the exchange can be done in one way or another. The first approach would take more resources and your return on risk will, therefore, be lower. Secondly, the same result can be obtained, but with less marginal resources.

Let's think about the first way.

You probably heard about a 'covered call.' You buy shares and write (or sell) call options for the same number of shares simultaneously. For example, in the US markets, it would be more than 100 shares.

The main element of this strategy is that written calling options are "in cash." You want the current stock market price at the time of entry to be above the strike price for call options.

Now the critical part is here.

You must ensure that the difference between the current market price of the underlying stock and the effect of the options purchased and sold is smaller than the credit earned from the above call/put setup. Do not forget to take account of the brokerage costs, which usually would be about $90 to enter and exit the trade.

That difference is your income. You can't lose money whatever happens from now on. Take an example to illustrate the argument.

An example to explain XYZ's current market price is $61.35. You buy 1,000 shares and at the same time sell $60 call option contracts at $4,90 or $4,900 premiums. You can buy 10 x $60 optional contracts for $3.10 per contract (so they are cheaper out of money) that cost you $3,100. The estimated debt is $1,800.

The disparity between option premiums above is $1.80, but between $61.35 and $60.00 is just $1.35. The 45 cents are now locked in income immediately, regardless of what happens afterward.

Let's assume that the share price has risen to $65 by the expiry date. Your purchased options will expire valuable and your sold call will lose $5,000. But your shares would benefit from $3,650. The disparity between the two is the loss of $1,350. But you got

$1,800 credit from your chosen strategy to make a net profit of $450 and raising brokerage costs.

By default, calling options are typically more costly than putting, because their inherent value for the future is infinite upside, while the intrinsic value of putting options can only vary from the present share price to zero. But if you consider something in the pricing option about implied volatility, you will consider it may not always be the case.

Looking at the above, you probably think $61.350 is a lot of money to invest in shares for a slight profit of $450 at optional expiration date.

Naturally, you'd be right-this is just about 1% return on investment. But what if the same outcome could be obtained without such a high cost? Will it be more appealing?

Recall, the only reason you purchased shares in the example above was to hedge your selling call options against risk. What if you could produce the same result, but with just around 5% of the spending?

There are other financial instruments that you can use to safeguard your position rather than purchasing securities, including future securities and CFDs.

For our reason, let us illustrate with differential contracts (CFDs). CFDs have no set "strike rates" such as optional contracts, so you will profit from these with long contracts of 1,000 XYZ for a difference of $61.35.

Why limit yourself to selling calls and buying items?

You may reverse the above structure, with the option often meaning volatility. In those situations why enter a CFD contract if the optional term is $58.65 and $58.650 plus interest is available to you to sell your 1,000 XYZ shares, then compensate for it with your sold $60 ITM option and hedge it with your bought OTM $60 call option.

Putting options are often more costly than calls because of increased implied volatility and are at the top of a trading range when the changeover is expected.

You will have to do some analysis for the above

strategy, like study the broker fees for the previous transactions and create a table to help you to evaluate the return on expenses quickly, after brokerage.

You'll want to make sure your broker accepts the long CFD contract as an appropriate protection against your "naked" sold call options for the cheaper approach by using CFD. In other words, a broker providing optional trading services alone cannot recognize your CFDs in another broker, so you may be interested in finding one broker providing both.

Finally, always know your broker fees at the expiry of entry and choice for the above. They are crucial in deciding how many choices you will join to make a profit.

CHAPTER 21

IS STOCK OPTIONS TRADING RISKY?

Most people agree that options trading is highly risky. After all, they buy a short-lived commodity and hope it gets worthwhile. Buyers with an option could make 500 percent or more if they buy the right choice as if they chose the winning horse on the track.

This is a little more time than a horse race to see if you are a major winner, but not much. When the stock does not go up in one month or two, you lose your total investment bet. Tear your ticket. Just tear up. You have selected the wrong team.

If the stock is down, the majority of option buyers also lose their full bet. Not surprisingly, people assume that selling options are risky. If you buy a stock, at least, you don't lose anything other than the opportunity to make a better investment.

It's a rising risk when you buy an option. It depreciates more quickly than a new vehicle. Within a matter of months, it is useless.

High risk, high reward – this is an investment reality that most people embrace. They believe that any program which offers extraordinary profits needs to involve an extremely high degree of risk.

When it comes to intelligent options trading nothing could be further from the facts.

I recall the legend of the blind men who looked at an elephant-that each man affected a single part of the animal and came to a completely different conclusion about what he reached. The two unequivocally accurate claims are seen as single transactions:

1) Buying stock options is highly risky.

In reality, buying stock options may be the risky form of investment that concerns most cautious investors. If we look at this small portion of stock market activity, we will appreciate that stock options entail high-risk investments.

2) The selling of stock options is much riskier.

When presented as a single trade, selling stock options is even worse! Selling an option alone is called selling it naked (because you feel like selling it all the time). You have the chance of unlimited risk. You will lose more money than you have spent several times. At least you lose the money you bet at the horse race.

No wonder people think that selling stock options is risky. All around there seems to be an extreme danger. Just like the blind men who examine the elephant, they look at only one part of the frame.

Because most people have not tried hard to understand stock options, they easily assume that the risk level for them is too high and put their money "free" like mutual funds. Somehow if they pay some "experts" to buy their own stocks, they delude themselves into thinking that they are prudently investing.

Nothing could be farther from the facts.

If your money is in a "free" investment fund, which is

the fact:

1), if stocks increase, you will make money (but management fees, distribution costs, and expenditures that are incurred will reduce your profits). The stock market has averaged around 10 percent a year for the past 50 years. It is the most benefit you can expect from investing in your mutual funds.

2) You lose money when the stocks stay flat (management fees and inflation the value of the holdings).

3) When inventories fall in value, you lose money.

Contrast these facts with a properly applied investment in stock options (as in the 10 K strategy I suggest):

1) If you increase the underlying stock, you make money, sometimes more than 100 percent a year.

2) You make money if the underlying stock stays flat, often at a rate of more than 100% a year.

3) You will also make a profit if the underlying stock

declines. You'll lose money even if the stock goes down a lot in a very short time. (In this case, of course, the mutual fund will also be clobbered.)

Which of the above two investments seem to be the riskiest? It seems to me that the investment in the mutual fund is a lot riskier than the investment in stock options (not to mention that the return on stock option portfolio will be just 1/10th).

Why then does the investment alternative have such a bad rap on the question of risk?

It is simply because people look at only one aspect of the picture (options to buy or sell) and disregard the entire picture.

They conclude that if the options for buying are risky, and selling options are even harder, the option trading will be twice risky. Most people do not consider a mechanism for buying and selling options simultaneously less risky than owning the stock. But most people never take the next step and know the facts. This is real.

The reality is that a successfully implemented stock options policy is much less expensive than a stock or mutual fund purchase. It takes time, however. You will have to think about the workings of options and be an active part of the investment process. You can't move your money like a mutual fund and neglect your investment passively.

The fact that buying stock options requires effort discourages most people even from considering buying in stock options. That's good with me. When I compare my returns with the results of the mutual funds last year, I feel like a real winner. I might work a little harder, but the reward for the returns I make is a small amount.

CHAPTER 22

THINKING "OUTSIDE THE BOX"

Would it not be nice if we could buy a five-month option until expiry and offer a 2-month option until the same price expires?

You could not lose that. Yeah, we can't. We can't. I love choices and I've realized something really interesting.

We can buy a spread with a lot of residual time value at about the same price as we can sell one with a lower value. The purpose opened my eyes and provided me with fresh perspectives. Here's what I know.

I started to compare how expensive the other strike rates were in the same month and the other months. Based on the price per day, I wanted to know which choices were more costly.

The first 1 or 2 months, as everybody knows, are

easily losing time value. The price of the money strike is very high relative to the price of the money strike. Since not so much time remains, how much will they charge for a money option? Not much. Not much.

The next few months will be the reverse. Compared with each other, the price per day strikes closer to the money are cheaper than the money alternatives. I would like to illustrate another way to use the S&P market.

The remaining six days at the cash option cost 12 points 6 days at the cash option cost 2 things 70 days remaining at the cash option cost 43 points 70 days out of the money option costs 29 points. There is more than 10 times the remaining time, but the money option 70 days (43 points) still costs less than 4X the money option price than the 6 days (12 points).

The 70-day out of money (29 points) is approximately 15x the expense of the six-day out of money (2 points), but the time is just 10X. We purchase the cheaper options per day and sell the more costly options per day.

Sell money for 6 days and sell the money for 70 days. Buy 6 days from the cash and buy 70 days from the cash. This is done for a debit of 4 dollars. We are now purchasing a 10X longer spread than the one we sell and are only charging 4 cents.

When the 6-day options expire, we will sell for additional premiums in the following month, while keeping the 70-day option.

What goes up must come down.

We have learned this about the laws of gravity before. We do have regulations in the energy markets. What's going down, will go up! The biggest traders like Warren Buffet of our time know this.

He could be the biggest stock trader ever. Until a few years ago, he had never traded goods. He bought silver on the market for the future. He purchased more as the economy went down.

The "smart money" and ads will not be afraid to sell when they have even more purchased a business. You know better than anyone that a product has real value and it is always worth it.

A popular book, "You Can't Lose Trading Commodities," is available. The author buys commodities and then waits for higher demand. He will buy more when the price fell. For this, you need a major bankroll. I know that maize isn't going to $1.00 but what if it did? If I want to end the trade, I want to reduce the risk.

This is how I began trading the Soy Complex a few years ago. It does not have choices.

Strictly future-oriented

I bought what had spread like a crush. I increasing the contracts as the market struggled against me before the distribution rebounded a little. I didn't need the business to return to where I started because I increased the contracts. It had only to bounce back to the next point.

This was done by Blackjack players before Casinos caught up and imposed caps on bets. It is understood that potential traders make good players and skilled gamblers make good traders for the potential. I'm against gambling, but it's not necessarily gambling even with a program.

The carders will bet on something like this: losing $5, losing $10, losing $20, losing $40, winning $80. The losses amount to 75 million. They will win 80 dollars and the benefit is five dollars. Not much, but they'd do it all day. Blackjack's chance for the match is just under 50 percent.

The problem is that you have a small chance of losing 40 times in a row. We now have a chance of 50 percent with commodities and can never lose 50 times in a row because the price cannot be below zero.

I will inform you now that I am not suggesting that you double your trade before I go any further. You can consider shares close to their lowest, where you can trade on a small scale. Spreads give even better chances. You have a closer (high to low) range.

At this moment you can see that we only do that for

a long time because we can never be sure how far demand will go. We must find a demand that is already low so that we don't have to wait too long, and then less capital is required.

I tend to use options to swap this. This can be achieved in many ways. In a market like soya, you could purchase an option and choose how many cents the price would drop before you purchase more. The question is that an alternative is a loss. The Theta (time decline) will make you lose money.

I use spreads and I don't have to account for the decay of time. I'll sell more Theta than I purchase, and I just make money on time if the market doesn't do anything.

CHAPTER 23

HOW TO GET MAXIMUM PROFITS IN LESS TIME ON YOUR OPTION TRADES

Most of the time, I like option trading because it rakes in premium profit. Indeed, they are responsible for selling the options (through organized businesses such as iron condors, butterflies, and spreads).

I assess this form of position when I believe the value of the option is higher and/or when I have a stock path. For example, if I have a bullish opinion about a stock, I might try to take advantage of high volatility options and sell spreads rather than paying for calls.

Another example of high volatility option ... offer a penny if it is a fairly low-price stock or if it is a high demand stock such as Priceline.com (PCLN) or Amazon.com (AMZN), it sticks to spreads.

Now, when it comes to profiting from this sort of

trade, I have strict guidelines that I obey. In comparison to long premium management trades, taking advantage of short premium trades is not as brown.

You will see that your profit potential and your risk have already been established when you apply a short premium option.

Until I get into it, I want to explain quickly how to make money on fast premium transactions.

1. Volatility alternative declining

2. The stock price will move (or not move much) in your favor

3. It is said that time decay options are wasting money

That said, we have no time decline item to worry about ... As we realize that time is still passing and choice decay is accelerating as expiry approaches. That said, we should concentrate on finding stocks with charts that we like and options with rich premiums.

How is it necessary to find stocks with high option

premiums?

That you can make money on the market several times if the stock doesn't move or even goes a little against you ... That's if the volatility option decreases.

Note, the higher the volatility option, the more expensive ... The cheaper options are the lower the volatility option.

For instance, the Trulia (TRLA) shares opened at $63.14 on 7/28/14 ... The $65 call in September (54 days expiry) opened for $6.20. The stock was sold up to $67.50 ... Yet those call options had a large print of $6.40.

Why can the stock be increased by $4, but just $.20 more than the opening price?

(Hint: This wasn't the decay of time) The volatility option decreased substantially ... Although stock moved upward-helping the calls-many of those gains were balanced by the decline in optional volatility.

So ...You're waiting for the right approach?

Mini Options - A Game Changer For Every Option Trader

For years, retail investors 'only options contracts were contracts that expired monthly or annually.

A new form of option with a weekly expiry date was introduced in 2010. New contracts expiring in eight days on the following Friday are valid every Thursday.

Traders able to determine the decline in time may use these weekly contracts separately or in combination with their monthly equivalent for their benefit. Today, only fewer than 200 businesses offer weekly options, but their popularity is growing and the phenomenon is sure to spread.

The next tease and commercial incentive for individual investors is the limited choice available next month. The mini-option governs only 10 percent of the subsidiary versus a conventional 1 option contract of 100 percent of the subsidiary stock or the subsidiary.

Initially, only a few highly traded, high-priced firms, such as Google, Apple, Amazon, and other ETFs have the mini-option available. S&P benchmark (SPY) and gold (GLD) are used in ETFs. When demand on the mini options begins to grow, the International Securities Exchange (ISE) starts selling the mini options.

The new mini options contracts start trading on all exchanges in a few weeks' time on 18 March. The demand should be high. Once, the divide between institutional and individual investors is further narrowed.

The introduction of these contracts seeks to open up the options market for smaller investors who have historically not been able to trade in a significant number of companies with share prices above $100 per share.

After surveys by brokerage companies revealed that many traders had the skills and experience required for trade options but lack the requisite account size to participate in the market, mini-contracts were introduced.

Take an investor who owns Google shares and

wishes to write covered calls to gain income by selling premium. This is not even probable when the buyer has one hundred shares on the stock market, equivalent to $80,000. The new mini options allow investors to own up to 10 shares, or a sum of $8,000, and to call for premiums on their smaller value.

A seasoned trader can and does produce consistent returns repeatedly using this covered call strategy. Mini options solve the dilemma for small traders who do not want to tie up capital into one hundred stocks.

Lotto Ticket Exchanges

Many individual players want to bet on names that are closely followed. For those with a certain name, they try to buy a call option before a trade reports its earnings. When the stock rises after the income announcement, big profits can be made. Playing lower-priced options against higher-priced stocks will yield huge profits in volatile inventories, such as Apple and Google, over a short time.

Using mini contracts, you will benefit from these

forms of lottery ticketing tours without having to gamble as much as you would with standard choices.

The latest mini options hit the market next month so that you plan for a great change in the demand for options. The area has just gotten much larger.

Mini options allow you to trade with less risk by establishing a smaller role than a standard option contract. It makes it much easier to handle the money properly with a smaller scale.

You may also diversify with more positions with smaller capital allocations. No single transaction absorbs a large portion of your portfolio and therefore reduces the risk of generating better chances.

The new mini options trade just like standard options, so please be careful when placing an order. Be sure whether you exchange the right trade and the right size or are over-extended.

Unfortunately, the latest mini options also come under the ludicrous SEC pattern day trader rules impacting accounts below $25,000. Be sure that you understand the rules or can suspend your account.

CHAPTER 24

ATTRIBUTES OF A SUCCESSFUL OPTIONS TRADER

After more than a decade as a qualified option trader and hedge funds manager, I was privileged to meet many of the world's leading option traders and to learn from the mistakes of thousands of broken option traders.

From the great courageous option traders who dared to go to where no one had before, and my own option trading experience, I am very excited to learn that the strategies used by both lucrative millionaire option traders and option traders are not so different.

Both types of option traders used the corresponding option strategies on the underlying asset path. Most of these option traders also have the same opinion about the same underlying asset but have drastically changed.

I gradually realized that a millionaire option trader needs more than just careful analysis and flawless option strategy execution. It takes another species of man! It needs a race of men whose attributes are not found naturally in most people and who act and think very differently from the average person.

I have compiled 5 outstanding qualities of real millionaire traders and have listed them here:

1. Cool

During the amplification of gains, option trading also amplifies the impact on the underlying asset with any slight whipsaw.

What looks like a tiny, harmless whipsaw in stock price can look like an earthquake in its options market. Met with a fast loss of a lot of money from whipsaws, a millionaire option trader stays cool and calm regardless of trading interest. So many option traders rescue and lose 50 to 60% of their capital instantly because of these whipsaws, as they are unable to keep calm in the face of these stresses.

I traded with one of my option trading students in the mid-2006 invitation options. This specific stock has gone into a quick and deep whipsaw that instantly took 50% of our positions.

The choice of trading my student almost went crazy and then sold the place that was losing even though we had yet to reach our stop loss point (it was then really close). That place gained me about 40% immediately after the whipsaw. The same trade, same opinion, different outcomes.

2. Patience

The stock market is not an auto-teller, but merely a withdrawal mechanism at will. No. No. The stock market is like an ocean, and we are all seafarers. Every seasoned sailor knows that you shouldn't go to sea for any season. This is the moment when veterans sit back and watch the amateurs die in the hurricanes.

A Millionaire Option Trader knows these seasons and has to wait until the harvest season, before traveling. Most amateur traders of options (yes, too), are interested in doing a lot of business rather than making profitable trades. Some would be in a rush and just sell, even if market conditions are too volatile to lead to a successful trade.

As we said, option trading greatly amplifies all whipsaws created by the underlying asset. In very turbulent times, when you reach the market, whipsaws are enough to frighten any option trader to make mistakes or to trick needless stop loss points.

A Millionaire Option Trader is like an addict; he swings and glides slowly, and if a strong chance emerges he leaps mercilessly to kill them.

3. Systematic

AMO is the systematic way to recognize trading possibilities, systematic trading and portfolio management, systematic execution of all trade, systematic stop-loss of any trade, consistent profit-making of all trade, systematic use of his or her lifestyle (to maintain a sound mind during hours of trade), systematic recovery of losses, etc.

Nothing is open to choices at the last minute. Nobody can be assured that under pressure, correct decisions will be made.

A Millionaire Option Trader does not decide at the time because all options and their operation have been scheduled beforehand. Unsystematic option traders, particularly in the field of commercial management, often have enormous losses and very small profits.

4. Organized

Not only are the disciplined millionaire option traders systematic, but they are also extremely organized traders. They adhere to their business plan, avoid loss points, and gain schemes with an iron-clad discipline regardless of how good or poor their situation is.

Discipline also ensures that millionaire traders are not driven by fear of failure or desire for gains. They only have one mission and that is to achieve their trading methods.

Unlike equity trading, the tremendous variance in

options also scares unruly traders to insensibly close their positions at large losses before their loss limits are reached and to take money off the table greedily when it is made even though their benefit requirements are not met.

It again generates a scenario where optional traders with the same perspective on the same stocks end up with very different outcomes by applying the same option strategies.

5. Most amateurs and traders of options frequently broke out by jumping from one trading system to another like the lost rabbit. They also convert from long-term option strategies to short-term investment trading simply because they believe there is money to make.

It is like the man who ordered steak for a minute, changed his order to pasta 5 minutes after that, and changed his order to burger before the pasta arrived. Both options trading require time to generate returns. One millionaire option trader insists on his account's trading and investment objectives and adheres to sensible approaches that achieve these targets.

There are several more attributes discrepancies between a millionaire option trader and a mauled option trader, but these are the key ones I think make a difference. Can this list help you focus on your own achievements or mistakes to make internal adjustments that demonstrate progress in trading with long-term options?

CHAPTER 25
TENETS OF DAILY TRADE DISCIPLINE IN OPTIONS TRADING

Whoever says that trading is "simple," is both untrained and lazy or is experienced, but is still lazy, and seeks to replicate a more inexperienced and lazy person. You need more than mantras to "Build and Acquire."

To ensure competitive trade outcomes, daily trade discipline must be cultivated. Like any other demanding career, the trading of online options from home is no different. Choose one tenet every month to learn. There are 12, so you have a year to gradually develop your skills.

1. Become a puritan award. The main explanation of why the price persists and adjustments are due to supply and demand. Where more purchasers have reasons for purchasing than sellers for selling, prices

will increase.

If more sellers have grounds to buy than buyers, then the price must decrease. Where buyers and sellers have fair or non-participation factors, the price will remain unchanged. This universal economic law is true of pure price trading techniques.

2. Dilute chance of concentration. S&P 500 accounts for just over 3/4 of market capitalization in the universe of mutual funds.

The top 100 stocks (with minor adjustments in inclusion/exclusion) in S&P 500 account for approximately 43 percent of what mutual funds are used to build their funds, which are the vast majority of mutual funds that hold the same stocks.

As the top 100 stocks are high, 2/3 of these funds are in large caps, with just one third preferring just small and / or medium caps. Big caps tend to have less relative strength than small and medium caps.

Market Diversification" was marketed to you-written on the marketing prospectus. But, despite the cap-weighted concentration, you are simply rising your exposure to weaker relative power, even though the big caps that you have are spread across sectors.

3. The theme-the junkie style-is "trendy." Fund managers typically remain in their style. An equity fund would not be a fixed-income fund. The charter of your business is predefined in the form of fund house you run.

A large growth fund remains a large growth fund even though large growth funds fail, whereas small and medium-sized funds are comparatively superior. It's not the fault of the fund manager, you funded the fund with your money.

This also explains in part why the high turnover of fund managers will affect the output of the fund, as the fund manager tries to change styles but is limited. Diversify what the news says is "Trendy" outside. Replace fund dependence by using optional Indexes / ETFs.

4. Limit the basics – the game of paper poker. The

investor psychology behind supply and demand is expressed exclusively in size, beyond basics. After the tragic 9/11 incident and the financial pandemic of 2008 that began in 2009, investors sold essentially sound stocks.

Benjamin F. King: Factoring in demand and industry; Business Journal, Jan. 1966: "Of stock fluctuations ... 20% is unique to one stock." Fundamental Analyst fuses with paper only to justify 20% of prices. As real as all FA jobs, will you play with the house armed with just 20% of the odds with analyst paperwork?

5. Divorce the fundamentals. You may think you are familiar with the commodity exchanged ("love" or "lust"). And you're looking for trends, configurations, signs that don't exist. Love is blind too.

It is more important to consider the cyclical/seasonal nature of the underlying asset class; and how the underlying complies with shifts in supply/demand with near-resistance rates. You don't even know the underlying. One underlying marriage imposes the burden of not swapping other more legitimate candidates. The stock does not "heart" you.

6. Then describe losses in advance of gains. ABOVE and Below risk reduction benefits AND as finite. However well-planned a trade is, it can never achieve its profit objective. Some opt for a 1% absolute trade capital loss rule to describe the absolute trade risk.

For example, if the trading capital is USD 50'000, 1 percent is equal to the maximum trade losses of $500; vs. 50% of the trade losses on the P / L of that particular position.

7. Doubling down speeds up losses. Just the total cost of the losses – known as 'catching a dropping knife' – is doubled. The breakeven continues as you chase the price. Trade for profit. Exchange for profit.

not trade even with odds against you for a split. Only add a winner if you replicate the setup of the original winning trade with entry conditions and Reward to Risk Ratio. Limit changes-has the sharpness of a knife ever been "adjusted?"

8. Keep the learning true and consistent thematically. Confront the obsession by learning from trades in which you have worked with "magical" tricks of "economic research wizards." Price signals are typically the best. Increase your insight into the price dimensions. Set 1%-2% of your portfolio for continuing self-education.

If you are struggling to relate it to any area or feature in a trading platform for whatever you know, unlearn it if you cannot relate what is learned to the price on the market. You will remove the "L" plate from "L" to receive.

9. Ditch the crutch of the app. Technology does not replace critical thought. Disrupt the machine logic (how, what, and why). Software Black Box cultivates a reliance on regularly unthinking subscriptions.

Break your habit, trust your intuition to reason- you've got profitable businesses you think about. When you "outsource" the trading-related administrative tasks (e.g. trading record), do not outsource your brain.

10. Plan business transactions with business discipline. Most plans contain entrances, exits, stops, and benefit goals. Still, with a few bullet points, no one enters a trade. Your trading strategy needs to trade with the very basic "Why trade?"

What motivates you (every day, month, and quarter)? For example, building a child education fund, paying for household expenses, or self-retirement? How robust do you want your home trade? This is reflected in the building of your portfolio and business plan.

11. Expectations unfounded. Slowly and steadily create wealth. Forget about the fantasy of hunting back there. Trading is a way of life. The markets will survive us all.

12. Scrooge-not smart, cheap.

Price efficiency is driven by volatility. Don't rely on the cost alone. Options on bid-ask alone are not reasonably priced. Options are based on what you are paying for them. For example, purchasing High(er)

Deltas may not be the cheapest but can offer the required directional variation. Rethink what you get for a certain amount of Theta decay.

As in real life, shopping for companies will lead to more junk than there is space to store. Don't end up with a junk call and position inventory in your portfolio. Get educated, get interested.

With a more rigorous day-to-day management, the features of a more consistent portfolio output should be obvious. Income will slowly increase according to the size of the account.

When it's in the ten thousands, the profits will slowly increase from the bottom hundreds to the higher hundreds, so they will increase from the top hundreds to the thousands. If your portfolio hits $100 K, income will grow from hundreds to thousands.

Profits from the lowest of hundreds to thousands signal excessive reliance on gap play, which does not allow you to continuously increase profitability.

CHAPTER 26
WAYS TO IMPROVE YOUR OPTIONS TRADING

Highlighted below are workable steps can be taken every day to boost the options trading.

1. Study and master options trading fundamentals

Before you start out and trade intermediate to advanced options, you must understand the basics of option trading. It's life's purpose. This is why we learn to do simple arithmetic and subtraction before we divide and multiply.

You need to learn more about "putting" and "calling" — how and when they work. This involves understanding all the links such as the expiry dates where they are found in the simple tables of choices. Simply playing over the basics of more sophisticated trading.

2. Technically, they don't have to be all about

options trading because every investment book overlaps.

The aim is to learn various approaches to market trading. You can think about stuff you hadn't learned before and may even refine your original trading strategy.

One interesting way to learn about book reading is that you can know more about the secret trading variables like investor psychology or market psychology you don't see every day. Do you know that the reasons why technological research occurs are these psychologies?

3. If you are analyzing six more technical metrics and using several technical analysis concepts against other technical analysis concepts, you are possibly doing a disservice to yourself. Only know and use elements such as MACD, support/resistance, trend channels, divergence/convergence, and moving averages.

4. Continue to Paper Trade

It does not mean that you have to stop studying and

try new tactics, simply because you are trading real money. You will continue to approach the market from every angle. If you adhere to the market (you prefer to follow the trend), try a counter-strategy. If you normally close credit spreads, try to hold one open as you put an OTM option.

Experiment and continue to change your plan

One great tip is to create 2 identical companies. One on your daily account and the other concurrently on your paper trading account. You can then make experimental changes over time to your paper account to see if it performs against the live account. This is a good way to check different techniques when you have a foundation.

5. Find a Trade option that you enjoy and master

A perfect way to improve your options trading is through the handling of a bread and butter trade. Re-tested historical data, check current conditions using paper trades, and read your favorite book trade. Learn all the ins and outside of your practice.

If you fully understand the intricacies of your business, you can better identify situations and markets in which your trade will expand. In addition, the probability of success and income is higher.

The trick is to stick to a simple business such as an iron cushion or credit distribution. No advanced trades stacked.

6. All successful traders have a trading plan. Stick to your trading plan

This means that they have a market plan, changes, and exit strategies based on Different events. Effective traders DO NOT arbitrarily make decisions. Everything they do is assessed, estimated, and analyzed. If you like, you can generate a simple trading formula based on technical analysis.

7. Wait for openings

For inexperienced traders, this is a big issue. It was also an issue for me when I began trading. I should have a couple of stocks on my watchlist, but I knew it wasn't the right time. And then the stock takes off when I don't look. I've chased stocks on a couple of occasions that eventually turned against me.

These types of circumstances hurt in two ways: 1) your ego teeth and 2) your welfare balance.

Don't worry if you have the same problems. Fortunately, it has been well established that, most frequently, good annual portfolio performance is due to a successful exit strategy.

8. Every business is a learning experience.

Log and learn from your previous trades. Don't only dwell on losing trades but look at the champions as well. Something you should still remember. For losing trades, see why the trade was lost or how likely it might have stopped. Analyze your entrance, your shifts, your departure, and your overall business behavior.

See why the trade won and potential ways you might have gained even more in winning trade. Analyze your entrance, the modifications, the departure, and the overall business behavior.

It's the same study for both forms of trades if you remember. After a few businesses, you'll start to understand the key features of why certain businesses succeed and why certain businesses fail. From there, you can see the changes that need to be made to minimize a loss or maximize income.

9. Learn from active traders who STILL Trade

While you have a mentor, you always look over your shoulder to make sure you set up the best possible trade for the present market. When you see them struggling with their own ideas, you will know that their advice is sound.

I consider it very strange to seek trading advice from someone not trading for themselves.

If you do not feel that you need continuing trading and support, ask yourself the following questions: • Why do professional athletes have their coaches?

- Why are Fortune 500 firms hiring consultants?

- Why would the President have consultants?

All these questions are answered with ease: mentors keep you accountable, help you to identify and accomplish your goals, look beyond, and provide a wealth of experience when trading with the subject matter. Mentors motivate you to become BETTER traders in theory.

If you are serious about options trading, it's worth your time today to check out any of these moves. The more you concentrate your skills and apply a laser focus, the easier it will be to find ways to make money on the market.

CONCLUSION

Most people assume that they should learn to trade options the same way they learned stock trading, which is just buying an option on stocks that they think will be successful. It's just that it's not simple?

Well, the simplicity ends when they realize that there is no choice but two and that either alternative has countless prices and expiry dates! That's right! That's right! You immediately remember that options trading is much more than stock trading.

Yeah, stock options are a different ball game from stock trading, even though they are used to benefit from moves made by stocks. Yeah, the fact that so many different strike rates and expiry dates are provided immediately shows you that there is no way to just pick up and make a profit.

less by trial and error attempt to learn. Yeah, trial and error in the options trading system are very expensive because you cannot hang on to a mistake like stock trading in the expectation of a return forever. Options expire so that options don't require you to keep up with your mistakes forever.

So, what's the best way to learn?

To learn how to exchange options, you must first learn what calling options and putting options are. All available inventories have both call options and position options. Call options allow you to buy a stock at fixed prices regardless of the price and provide options for the selling of stock at fixed prices regardless of the price of stock.

If you buy a call option and the stock price rises, the call option will make a profit, as you will have the right to purchase at a rate lower than the stock price. As such, if you think a stock would increase, you can buy call options. On the other side, you can use options to sell a stock at a fixed price.

And if you purchase a placement option and the stock price falls, the placement option would make a profit because you will have the right to sell at a cost greater than the stock price. As such, you'd buy options if you thought a stock would go down.

This is just a quick description of what call and place choices are so you start thinking about choices.

If you have a good picture of call options and placement options, you must know what rates and expiry dates are. The price negotiated in an options contract is a strike price.

A $10 strike price call allows you to buy a stock at $10 regardless of the stock price, and a $10 strike price fixed option allows you to sell stock at $10 regardless of what stock price is.

Streak prices cover a very large variety of prices both higher and lower than the current stock price. That takes us to the next important thing to know about options; Money options.

Depending on the strike price, either in the market, in the market, or in out of the money, may be an option. Ways of different money supply various viewpoints.

You'd buy the cash options if you think that a stock makes a major move and buy the money options when only a fairly small move is predicted. In comparison to stock trading, where you only buy the stock if you think it will go up, options trading lets you think about the potential degree of movement to maximize profit.

Total knowledge of money options and the effect of money options cannot be done without knowing how pricing options are dependent on their intrinsic value and their extrinsic value.

You cannot intelligently select the best choice for your particular viewpoint by simply knowing the difference between intrinsic value and external value and how to determine how much of each value is in the option price.

Once you understand what calling and placing options are, the prices, and the consequences of different money, it's time to learn how to position orders through your option broker.

Placing orders for options, since there are four primary types for options trading, unlike the two basic order forms for trading stocks.

Buy to open lets you open a new options position by purchasing it, selling to open lets you open a new options position by creating and selling a new options contract, buy to close lets you buy back and close options that you created and sold to sell and conclude lets you sell options that you previously purchased.

Knowing precisely what such instructions do is incredibly necessary to know how to execute highly complicated options.

Yes, option strategies let you take advantage of several directions and consider many more broad viewpoints, and it is one of the most unique features of options trading. The combination of long and short options creates strategies that go beyond merely profiting whether a stock goes up or down.

There are hundreds of thousands of options and some are so complicated that one position is made up of four to eight different trades using a complex combination of the various order types that you have mastered. Each alternative strategy is a study alone that takes a long time to know how to trade.

You can begin placing a few basic option trades after you have learned all of the above and know exactly what you are doing. See how often you know to exchange your first options?

Yes, options for trading require investments that go beyond buying and selling and are just as much a science as an art. Follow the steps above, do your due diligence and all of you will be prepared for your first choices.

www.ingramcontent.com/pod-product-compliance
Lightning Source LLC
Chambersburg PA
CBHW071357210526
45465CB00001B/137